Rooted in God's Grace

The Bible Reading Fellowship
15 The Chambers, Vineyard
Abingdon OX14 3FE
brf.org.uk

The Bible Reading Fellowship (BRF) is a Registered Charity (233280)

ISBN 978 0 85746 587 0
First published 2018
10 9 8 7 6 5 4 3 2 1 0
All rights reserved

Acknowledgements
Unless otherwise acknowledged, scripture quotations taken from The Holy Bible,
New International Version (Anglicised edition) copyright © 1979, 1984, 2011 by
Biblica. Used by permission of Hodder & Stoughton Publishers, a Hachette UK
company. All rights reserved. 'NIV' is a registered trademark of Biblica. UK trademark
number 1448790.

Scripture quotations taken from *The Message*, copyright © 1993, 1994, 1995, 1996,
2000, 2001, 2002 by Eugene H. Peterson. Used by permission of NavPress. All rights
reserved. Represented by Tyndale House Publishers, Inc.

Scripture quotations taken from the Holy Bible, New Living Translation, copyright ©
1996, 2004, 2007, 2013. Used by permission of Tyndale House Publishers, Inc., Carol
Stream, Illinois 60188. All rights reserved.

Every effort has been made to trace and contact copyright owners for material used
in this resource. We apologise for any inadvertent omissions or errors, and would
ask those concerned to contact us so that full acknowledgement can be made in
the future.

A catalogue record for this book is available from the British Library

Printed and bound by CPI Group (UK) Ltd, Croydon CR0 4YY

HANNAH FYTCHE

Rooted in God's Grace

Dwelling in the knowledge of God

To God – who is immeasurably kind,
always present and overwhelmingly life-giving –
and to all those who long to find their home in him.

Contents

Foreword

To write with simultaneous simplicity and depth is a skill which eludes many established writers. In this honest mix of *lectio divina*, spiritual autobiography and prayerful advice, Hannah Fytche proposes a vision of Christian discipleship which is authentic and attentive to the realities of human life rooted in the overwhelming reality of God's gracious, providential and relentless generosity. The narrative here is one of Easter, and of the summons to the Christian to enter into the Paschal Mystery. But this is a book at once homely as well as profound; around the 500th anniversary of the beginning of the Lutheran reformation, Christians from many traditions have been pondering afresh what it might mean to be rooted *sola fide et sola gratia*, that fundamental insight of Paul that it is only by faith alone, by grace alone, that we are grafted into the saving work of Christ. Hannah's answer to these questions is to learn how to accept the gift of redemption, truly knowing yourself redeemed, loved, overwhelmed by grace and thus transformed for Christian action.

The heart of this book is a great encouragement to a deeper relationship with Christ, honed in prayer and learned by heart. Scripture, silence, the curiosity awoken in prayer – none of these is something to be afraid of. Rather, in embracing the journey of discipleship, with all its inevitable ups and downs, we learn further how to receive the gift. Not through striving, as if we could ever achieve this alone, or fulfil some kind of imposed necessary criteria. But rather in an honest joy which seeks Christ with all our heart, soul, mind and strength. Hannah invites us to a shaped life, a life which is patterned on the shapes of scripture and liturgy, and on the friendship we discover with fellow pilgrims en route. We call that pilgrimage the church, a dynamic place, where we are inspired by our Christian ancestors as well as our contemporary sisters and brothers; a place where, as Hannah puts it, we encounter 'diverse unity, boundless love and risky faith' as we 'remind each other of the grace of Christ'. This is a vision which can re-enchant our communities, and which encourages us to trust that if we are rooted in Christ we will indeed grow up, gradually, imperceptibly, even 'into the full stature of Christ' (Ephesians 4:13).

Revd Dr Jamie Hawkey
Dean of Clare College, Cambridge
Chaplain to H.M. The Queen

Like a tree planted by water

Over the last few years, in whispers like zephyrs, God has spoken to me in these ancient words from the book of Jeremiah:

> But blessed is the one who trusts in the Lord,
>   whose confidence is in him.
> They will be like a tree planted by the water
>   that sends out its roots by the stream.
> It does not fear when heat comes;
>   its leaves are always green.
> It has no worries in a year of drought,
>   and never fails to bear fruit.
>
> JEREMIAH 17:7–8

The picture that's painted here is vital, vibrant and full of life, and within it there's a promise. It's a promise from God that's firm and true: that he will make something beautiful out of people who choose to trust and hope in him, wherever they find themselves in life. As I type these first few words, and as you read them, let's dwell on this image for a while. Let it become the promise against which the rest of this book will unfold.

Blessed is the one who trusts in the Lord, whose confidence is in him.

Blessed is the one who gazes towards God and has him as their vision. When things are shaky, blessed is the one who makes God their author. Blessed is the one who lets God write their story and give them confidence – confidence that is unwavering and firm, not based on performance, feelings or circumstance, but based on the never-failing, powerful-heart-beating love of God.

They will be like a tree planted by the water that sends out its roots by the stream.

This is the most beautiful image for trust. As we find our confidence in God, we become like a tree. It sounds a bit strange when written so bluntly but, in reality, it is a stunning simile to use.

The increase of trust in God is like the growth of deep roots. To trust is to become like a tree with roots growing deep down into cool water, streams of God's grace running fast and free. Our roots draw up the sustenance we need to thrive; God provides the grace and strength we need to grow.

It does not fear when heat comes; its leaves are always green.

With roots buried deep in the grace of God, the tree grows. It grows fearless and brave in the face of scorching heat – as the sun blazes down, the leaves defiantly stay green and lush. By the grace of God, they do not wither or turn crackly and brown – they rustle with life rather than death.

When we trust God, he upholds us and breathes life into us even when we're pressured or persecuted or feeling worn down to the bone. He breathes strength so that we persevere and 'rustle' with life always, like evergreen leaves.

It has no worries in a year of drought and never fails to bear fruit.

Even in times of drought, the tree doesn't need to worry. There are deeper springs that give it the water it needs and living springs bubbling up to everlasting life. This water allows the fruit to swell into abundance.

When it feels dry and desert-like, either because of difficult circumstances or because we feel distant from God, we must keep trusting our Father. When we keep trusting and walking by faith rather than sight, we can be certain that we will have the water – the grace – that we need. When we trust God, he will bring life. Fruit will grow.

At the start of my second university year, I found myself in a desert-like place. Not literally – my university town is still there and thriving, not sandy and desolate! But inside, I felt like I was in a desert. There were days where I had completely had enough – had enough of trying to pray and feeling like I was getting absolutely nowhere. I didn't know why and it was exhausting.

I've come to describe this time by using Elijah's story in 1 Kings 19. This was the story I opened my previous book, *God's Daughters*, with, and it's a story I've oft-returned to over the past few months. Elijah stood up for God radically and bravely. Despite powerful opposition, he preached against the kingdom's practice of idol worship, showing that God was the true God by bringing down fire from heaven (you can read this story in 1 Kings 18). Having disproved and captured the prophets of the false god, Baal, Elijah's life is in danger – and so he runs hard from his pursuers and ends up in the desert. He lies down in exhaustion under a scratchy broom bush. He's had enough, and he lets God know about it.

On hearing Elijah's cries for an end to his life, God (beautifully) doesn't tell Elijah to get up, man up and plunge back into the fray. He doesn't pluck Elijah out from under the broom bush and dust him off, send him back out. Instead, he listens.

He listens to Elijah's needs and responds to them. He gives Elijah food and water, sustenance for his worn-out body. Then, responding to Elijah's greatest need, he takes him on a journey. Elijah needs to walk through the wilderness and learn to long for God with hope, to pursue God with faith even when he feels downhearted.

So, God takes Elijah on a journey, leading him into the wilderness and keeping him there for 40 days.

The number 40 in the Bible symbolises struggle. Noah endured 40 days in the ark; the Israelites searched for their homeland for 40 years; Jesus spent 40 days in the desert being tempted. Elijah, in his weariness and grief over his plight, is given the gift of 40 days of struggle too.

It is a gift because it gives Elijah space to long with the certain hope of the most compelling vision: God himself. And it's even more of a gift because God was in this with him, sustaining him. I conjecture this, but with reason: Elijah started his journey with food given by God and ended it by hearing from God on the mountain. God must have been in the middle, too, sustaining Elijah along the way.

I think we all have these wilderness times in our lives, times where we long to see God but find it really difficult. We may not know why and it's really hard – but it's also a reality. For me, the hardest part of these times is knowing how to keep walking through the wilderness, and how to keep growing roots in God's grace even when it feels like a monumental effort with no reward. We can be encouraged by knowing that God is walking *with* us – we do not seek him alone.

The question is: how can we learn to walk in this knowledge that God is *with* us, even in difficult times? What do we do to keep going with God in the wilderness?

If you've grown up around Christians or you are a Christian yourself, you'll know the obvious answers: read the Bible and pray! These are the two top answers wherever you are in life, and rightly so. But I've realised that, while it's easy to say, 'Ah yes! We must read the Bible and pray!', it's infinitely harder, of course, to *actually* pray and read the Bible – particularly in a way that satisfies the soul.

Myriad questions swirl around inside my head as I come to 'spend time with God'. How do I read the Bible well? Where should I start – with Genesis, a gospel or something really obscure like Habakkuk? What words should I use to pray? Is it okay to ask God for things? Why are prayer and the Bible so good anyway? And the biggest question of all: why on earth do people call it 'quiet time', when sometimes I want to shout loudly at God?

I'm sure that you'll have asked these questions before, or questions like them. Take a moment to jot your queries down somewhere – on a sticky note, in the margins, in a notebook. Refer back to them as you're reading this book. I hope, in the following chapters, to start to answer some of them – or spark your thoughts so you can answer them yourself.

I'm not an expert on prayer or the Bible, just someone who's on the same journey as you: the journey of trying to grow roots in God's grace and follow him meaningfully and riskily. I won't be able to give you perfect answers, and I won't be able to solve struggles in your own prayer life. I simply hope to share some simple and practical stories of my own and, in doing so, help and encourage you to keep going! Seek his face always; it's worth it.

With these hopes in mind, here's how the book will unfold. We'll start with the truths we are rooted in as God's children. By grace we belong to God. We are precious in his sight and he delights in us just as he delights in his Son; he calls us his own. He made us and he redeemed us – and he promises to be with us always. How do these fantastic, startling truths shape how we pray? We'll explore this question in Section I.

Section II will be a practical uncovering of rhythms which can help us to become ever-more rooted in God's truths. We'll discuss the value and practice of everyday faithfulness, placing specific rhythms of rootedness – Bible study, prayer, experiencing creation, dwelling in silence or rest and being a part of church – within the context of such faithfulness.

In the chapters of Section II, we'll look at why each rhythm can be helpful and what we can do to practise it. I'll pack them full of creative suggestions and stories for you to be inspired by – just remember that each suggestion is exactly that: a *suggestion*. I'm not writing a checklist for you to live your life by; my aim is to provide you with ideas and stories which give you the passion and confidence to pursue God in your own way.

To this end, there'll be questions to help you think through these rhythms and truths at the end of each chapter. I've called this 'headphones time', a phrase borrowed from a friend of mine who was my youth worker a few years ago. She once said to me that I needed to put headphones in – not to listen to louder music, but to block out other noise and listen only to God's voice. You can use the questions I've put together to help you with this if you'd like.

Finally, scattered throughout Section II you'll find 'story stops', little interludes in which I've written stories from different points in my life. These – as well as being a bit of fun – are there to illuminate the main chapters by looking at past experiences which have formed and influenced my thoughts about knowing God. As you read them, take a few moments to think back on your own life. What memories or moments do you have that offer you glimpses of God's grace?

With that roadmap, I think we should begin – and begin with a prayer. This is my prayer for me as I write this book, and for you as you read it. Take a moment to turn to our God.

Father, may your Spirit fill us with hunger for you.

Inspire us to pray with your passion, the joy of your presence
motivating us and your will sustaining us. Let us lay down our
own agendas and aims.

Give us fresh vision of the fruit you want to bring from our lives.
Teach us to be rooted deep in you and help us to make space
to listen to you.

Make us radically confident in you. Help us to know Jesus and
joyfully follow his voice without comparing ourselves to
others. May we keep our eyes fixed only on you as you write
our stories.

Father, bring us to full, vibrant, world-changing life as we find
ourselves in you.

In your everlasting, heart-beating-love, grace-running-wild
name,

Amen

SECTION I

Truths to be rooted in

1

The story

I had always felt life first as a story: and if there is a story, there is a storyteller.[1]

Sunlight poured through stained glass, soft green light sparkling with brightest gold. It spilled on to old pews and painted walls; it rippled over the heads of the congregation. At the front, Ellie was speaking, full of passion and love for God. She was preaching a New Year's sermon titled 'Rooted in relationship with God'. Having just begun to write this book, I was amazed simply by the coincidence of that one phrase. I was struck even more by the words that she spoke: 'To be rooted in relationship with God, start from the knowledge that he's already given his all to us.'

He's already given his all to us. I jotted these words down, captivated by the truth – and thankful for how perfect the words were for the start of this chapter. He has given his all, everything, nothing held back. The Father heart of God beat love for us so wild that he stopped at nothing; he poured out everything, even to death.

And because he gave everything, there is nothing we need – or are able – to give, apart from our response in love to him.

The message of these words may be one you're familiar with already. Jesus came to earth and died for us, so that we could be with God and God with us, despite everything we've done wrong. The words fall from my pen with familiarity, running so deep that it's easy to forget the excitement, hard to pause in awe.

Ellie, as she preaches, does not forget. In her eyes are real joy and hope, and her voice rises with passion and praise.

Our God is with us! The Creator of the universe is in our midst. The one who breathed the stars into being, who understands the workings of the smallest cell, who knows our deepest dreams and fears – he is with us, near and here. We could list aspects of who he is for hours and years, and still not reach the end. This is the God who is with us, close enough to whisper and powerful enough to roar.

Isaiah knew this as he wrote the words we find today in Isaiah 40. These words clearly fell with awe on to his page as he reflected on the greatness of God. 'Who has measured the waters in the hollow of his hand, or with the breadth of his hand marked off the heavens?' (v. 12), the poet asks, implying that it is only God who could answer affirmatively.

Next time you're at the beach, scoop up some of the ocean's cold water in the hollow cup of your hands. Try to hold it there – and gaze out at the rest of the sea. The approximately 70 millilitres that your hands are struggling to contain are nothing compared to the 1.3 billion cubic kilometres of water in the world's oceans. God's hands can hold these oceans.

When it gets dark, look up at a clear night's sky. 'Lift up your eyes and look to the heavens: who created all these?' says Isaiah (v. 26). The stars glitter from light years away as we crane our necks, gaze upwards and try to locate constellations we only vaguely know. We can't even begin to count the pinpricks of light up there on the canvas of the sky; yet God brings them out 'one by one and calls forth each of them by name' (v. 26).

In the book *Indescribable*, Matt Redman writes: 'Stars in all their furious and explosive glory contain the unrivalled power of a mighty Creator.' He reflects on how space travel and research continually reveal how much more there is out there that we cannot see, encounter or comprehend – the silver sparkles of starry sky that are visible from earth are but 'tiny echoes of the might of who he really is. The faintest whispers of his thunderous power and strength.'[2]

The light that reaches us is just a tiny whisper of all that is out there. The most enchanting photos of the Milky Way merely hint at the full glory of the universe – 'These are but the outer fringe of his works; how faint the whisper we hear of him! Who then can understand the thunder of his power?' (Job 26:14).

We catch at the edges of his glory.

All we know is that God's power, strength and beauty extend further than we can imagine, thundering with incomprehensible majesty. God is big enough to cup the oceans in his hands; he is vast enough to create galaxies upon galaxies further away than we can ever hope to see.

Chapters 38—41 of the book of Job, similarly to Isaiah 40, contain a litany of questions which all point to the incomparable power and sovereignty of God. These questions spiral near the end of the story of Job's suffering, suffering caused by severe illness and extensive loss. Job wants to know why God has let these things happen, calling on God to come and answer for his actions. Like anyone who has encountered the dark things of the world, Job wants to understand the reasons *why*. Yet, instead of answering Job's question directly, God unexpectedly asks: 'Who is this that obscures my plans with words without knowledge?' (Job 38:2).

From here, God's voice spins into question after question:

> Where were you when I laid the earth's foundations?
>   Tell me, if you understand.
> Who marked off its dimensions? Surely you know!
>   Who stretched a measuring line across it?
> On what were its footings set,

or who laid its cornerstone –
while the morning stars sang together
and all the angels shouted for joy?
JOB 38:4–7

In such fast-paced poetry, the questions of God continue, asking about how oceans were separated from lands; where the origins of light, dark and sea reside; who commands rain to fall and lightning to strike; whether Job knows when, where and how the mountain goats give birth.

Job cannot answer and God's questioning continues. God's knowledge and power are overwhelmingly evident, his presence over all of creation implied and described.

At the end of this demonstration of God's great power, Job is awestruck. He takes back his demand to know why, because he realises that to know the reasons for his suffering would be to comprehend God – and, as his inability to answer God's questions has shown, no human could ever comprehend something so incomprehensible. He humbly acknowledges the awesomeness of God:

I know that you can do all things;
    no purpose of yours can be thwarted.
You asked, 'Who is this that obscures my plans without
    knowledge?'
    Surely I spoke of things I did not understand,
    things too wonderful for me to know.
JOB 42:2–3

Beyond the visible fringes and edges of glory is a God who is unimaginable, holding things too wonderful for us to know. There is a God who is incomparable, vast in his power and might, and dazzling in his creativity and beauty. There is a God that our words cannot capture, that our minds cannot contain, that no amount of study or effort will ever pin down. We stand at the threshold of the unimaginable and crane our necks to see – and we stumble back, amazed just to glimpse a spark merely reflected from the light of God's presence. Beyond the edges of glory: it is here that words fail. It is here that we fail.

To think of God in this way inspires awe and worship. But it can also be scary as we think about how big God is and how small we are. Redman, again in *Indescribable*, tells a story of a taxi driver whom he was speaking to about the immense brilliance of the stars. The driver asked him to stop speaking, saying, 'I try not to think about these things… the sheer scale of things totally unnerves me. It's just too big. It makes me feel so afraid.'[3]

If we had no knowledge of God, I expect that we too would be afraid by the immensity of it all. Even knowing God, we could be scared by his power, totally overwhelmed by his unstoppable strength. There is a reason that some of Jesus' first post-resurrection words to his followers were 'Do not be afraid' (Matthew 28:10).

Our God is mighty, yet the command of Jesus is 'Do not be afraid'. We as God's children have nothing to fear. This is because we know of his great love for us as well as his mighty strength: because he loves us, we do not have to be terrified before God. Humble, yes, and fearing God like Job feared God, yes – but terrified, no.

This is because we know that Jesus died and rose again. He fulfilled God's promises to save his people and we know from this that we are safe, loved and given new life. The strength and beauty God displays in starry skies and ocean depths are combined with overwhelming compassion – and this means that, in Ellie's electrifying words, he gives his all to us. We can stand amazed and wonderstruck, because God has revealed to us his love as well as his strength.

Before we explore this a little more, put down this book and close your eyes. Reflect on the following words from the Bible, and pray that God's Spirit – God himself with us – would come and show you more of who he is and how much he loves his people. Take as long as you want. These are the words:

> The Lord your God is with you,
>   the Mighty Warrior who saves.
> He will take great delight in you;
>   in his love he will no longer rebuke you,
>   but will rejoice over you with singing.
>
> ZEPHANIAH 3:17

Now you've had time to pause and wait in the unimaginable presence of God, dwell on just one word of this verse: 'with'. It's an incredible word, especially when put in the context of God and 'you', his people, us. The awesome Creator of the universe, the one who is beyond the edges of glory, *with* us?

I realised the beauty of 'with' just before beginning the university term one January. I was away on a student week of prayer, worship, conversation and fun. Among all this, my highlights were good food, lots of sleep, a sprinkle of snow and a wealth of encouraging conversations with friends. It was in one of these conversations that Rachel introduced me to the humble words of Job that I quoted above, and showed me more of what it means to be *with* God.

The two of us – Rachel and I – had been speaking about the previous term and the Christmas break, and what God had been speaking to us about. We'd both had tough times; God was teaching us both about his goodness. It was in this context that Rachel spoke of Job. She read the verses from chapter 42, and then said: 'Last term it's like I'd had faith that was trying to hold on to God by my fingertips, like Job had tried to understand God's purposes in suffering. God's shown me that I don't need to hold on by my fingertips because he holds me in the palm of his hand.'

We don't need to hold on by our fingertips. We don't need to strive after knowledge of God. We don't need to know everything about him – and as we've seen, we can't! All that God asks of us is that we sit in the palm of his hand and know that he knows everything, that he loves us and has chosen us, and that he is *with* us, always.

The rest of this chapter is going to look more at what it means to be 'with' God, a God of incomparable power and generous love. To do this, we'll explore the story, told by Paul in Ephesians 2:1–10, that shows us the truth of who we are as we choose to turn to God, listen to his voice and fall into the palm of his hand. Before we start, have a read of those Ephesians verses.

As you read through those words, you might have recognised them as describing your own story – a story of being brought from death to life, from darkness to light, from a place of punishment to a space of forgiveness. Even if you wouldn't call this narrative your own, I hope that reading these verses gave you a glimpse of what the core of Christianity is: a curiosity to read on, and perhaps even a desire to see yourself included in this tale.

For it is an amazing tale of redemption: being made to be with God when once we were without him.

Paul tells this story in the context of a letter to the Ephesian church. This church was thriving and flourishing in God's love; Paul's purpose in recounting their redemption story was to encourage them to praise together the God who gave them life. He thus tells the story retrospectively, giving the church a written reminder of the roots of their identity as God's children.

The first three verses describe where the Ephesians, and where we all, start from in this tale:

> As for you, you were dead in your transgressions and sins, in which you used to live when you followed the ways of this world and of the ruler of the kingdom of the air, the spirit who is now at work in those who are disobedient. All of us also lived

among them at one time, gratifying the cravings of our flesh and following its desires and thoughts. Like the rest, we were by nature deserving of wrath.

While typing out these words, I am hit by the harsh nature of such a description. Cast your mind back to the first part of this chapter, where we glimpsed the incomparable power of God through the words of Isaiah and Job. This is the God we stand before: mighty in strength; essentially good and just; mysterious beyond our comprehension.

Before this God, who could stand – especially those who have arrogantly tried to place their own wisdom above God's? The author of Job realised that people cannot understand the purposes of God, describing human theories and speculations as 'words without knowledge' (38:2). Isaiah's poetry captures this sense of futility as well: 'All people are like grass, and all their faithfulness is like the flowers of the field. The grass withers and the flowers fall… but the word of our God stands for ever' (40:6–8). In Isaiah's words, people are like 'grass' which inevitably falls, fades and is blown away, forgotten.

Paul's words to the Ephesians are just as punchy. He describes those who are disobedient to God as 'dead in… sins' and 'deserving of wrath', obedient not to the voice that spoke to Job out of the whirlwind but obedient to other voices, voices that promise worth based on standards other than the truth of God – standards such as our own wisdom, strength, intelligence, beauty, wealth or popularity. Although pursuing these standards might seem easier, more fun or more personally advantageous, it's actually a symptom of forgetting who we are – we seek to achieve and appease these other standards when we've forgotten that we're made in the image of God and that we are already loved, held, accepted and enough in his eyes. We place our own agendas above his, walking in the 'ways of this world' with a proud attitude that says, 'I can do it all, I don't need God. My worth is secure in things other than his love. My own strength is enough.'

We are not rooted in God's grace when this is our attitude. Trying to create our own worth and live off our own strength uproots us completely, teaching us to listen to deceptive voices that promise much but reward little. Jeremiah captures this in the following verses:

> Cursed is the one who trusts in man,
>   who draws strength from mere flesh
>   and whose heart turns away from the Lord.
> That person will be like a bush in the wastelands;
>   they will not see prosperity when it comes.
> They will dwell in the parched places of the desert,
>   in the salt land where no one lives.
> JEREMIAH 17:5–6

(You might like to compare these with the partner verses that follow in vv. 7–8, with which I opened this book.)

To trust in our own 'flesh' or strength might seem attractive and good – but really, it is to follow the ways of this world; it is to turn away from God and become like 'a bush in the wastelands' rather than 'like a tree planted by water'.

Ephesians 2:1–3 is thus a harsh description of uncomfortable truths, truths that confront us with our own sense of weakness and wrongdoing in the face of God's might and justice. Like Matt Redman's taxi driver, we might just want to stop thinking about it or we might be too afraid to continue. When I read these verses, particularly as they are written so directly and inclusively with words like 'you', 'we', and 'our', I feel like I'm looking in a mirror that shows up the darkness that resides in my heart – the attitude which rears its ugly head in the moments where I choose to ignore God and follow what I think is right, even when God is telling me it's wrong.

These verses confront my pride, apathy and arrogance, and I can only kneel, face buried in my hands, unable to look as my heart tremblingly acknowledges that God is holy and I am not. I pray for you to have courage to look in the mirror too, for knowing who we are without God leads us to a greater understanding of who we are *with* him. In writing these hard words, then, I do not intend to scare or guilt-trip you. I mean, following Paul's telling of the tale, to reveal reality and the background for the amazing thing that happens next.

What happens next is described in Ephesians 2:4–5: 'But because of his great love for us, God, who is rich in mercy, made us alive with Christ even when we were dead in transgressions – it is by grace you have been saved.' A brilliant shaft of light breaks powerfully into the darkness of guilt and wrath explored in 2:1–3. From my kneeling position, my face rises from my hands and my eyes look up. Before me is not a powerful, holy God who I am separated from because of my sin, but a powerful, holy God who I can be with because of Jesus. Radiant with God's glory, Jesus draws near and makes God close to me, saying in a beautiful, strong and compelling voice: 'Come.'

God, through Jesus, breaks into our habitually disobedient living, reaching down into our 'death' and choosing to make us 'alive'. Dwell on that for a moment, that transition from *death* to *life*. It's huge! Do you see it? Where once we were distant from God, we are now able to draw close to him. Where once we travelled the path to wasteland destruction, we now are given new life, purpose and strength to follow God's ways and become like trees planted by water. Where we once were *dead*, we are now *alive*.

In verse 5, Jesus is named as the one who moves us from distant-from-God death to able-to-draw-near life: God 'made us alive *with Christ*'.[4] It is with, through and all because of Jesus Christ that we can be with God. This is the centre of our faith: Jesus. Jesus, through whom all things were created (Hebrews 1:2). Jesus, to whom centuries of prophecy look in the hope that God will redeem his people (Luke 24:25–27). Jesus, in whom God came to earth to bring new life (John 1:4, 10–13). All three of these statements about Jesus are completely awe-inspiring, yet do not even scratch the surface – we could spend years exploring who Jesus is and still not know him completely.

It is the last of these that Paul focuses on in Ephesians 2:5 when he says that we have been 'made… alive with Christ'. Elsewhere, Paul writes, 'I have been crucified with Christ and I no longer live, but Christ lives in me. The life I now live in the body, I live by faith in the Son of God, who loved me and gave himself for me' (Galatians 2:20). It's hard to know exactly what Paul means here – he has not been literally crucified with Christ! I think the sense of what Paul is saying is that, unlike his old self, the habits which once formed him now no longer define him. He realised that the standards he lived by were not God's standards and he therefore let them be 'crucified' with Christ. Christ dies and rises, and gives Paul a new identity: the 'I' that Paul once was, comprising beliefs (like the belief that you had to follow the Mosaic law to be right with God) and consequent practices (like persecuting the church), no longer matters to him; he identifies totally with Jesus.

He can identify and be with Jesus because Jesus 'loved me and gave himself for me'. The simplicity of this phrase is beautiful as it points directly and dependently to the death of Jesus Christ on the cross.

Jesus loved Paul, and loved us, even when we were 'dead' in our sin, even when we were choosing to trust in beliefs (like the belief that having, being or doing more will bring us life, worth and salvation) and practices (like competing to 'get ahead' in order to prove ourselves) that are against God. He loved us so much that he 'gave himself for' us, emptying himself and stepping down from heaven to walk on the earth. On earth, he walked to the cross and he endured pain, mocking, torture and humiliation so that he could also endure the wrath of God in our place. *We* were the ones 'deserving of wrath', Paul writes to the Ephesians, but *Jesus* took what we deserved, dying in our place. *He* took the punishment for our sin. And how great that punishment must have been – think once more about the words in

Isaiah and Job, and how powerful God is. The punishment Jesus took for us was backed by this power and this standard of justice.

Having borne the weight of our sin, Jesus lay cold in a grave for three days. And then he was raised to life and was made alive again! He gained victory over death and over the paths leading to death; he walked the surface of the earth once more and he said to his disciples, 'Do not be afraid.'

Do not be afraid – because he gives us this life too. We are 'made… alive with Christ' (Ephesians 2:5): death and wrongdoing no longer have a grip on us and we are no longer 'deserving of wrath'. We are 'raised… up with Christ' (Ephesians 2:6)! We are alive with him!

I think on this and… *wow*! From my position of kneeling, I now stand with eyes totally fixed on Jesus. He looks at me, challenging, purifying, transforming and *loving* me. I am alive and I walk forward and with me is God's Spirit, his Spirit sent by Jesus crying out 'Father', his Spirit that marks me as his child. This is a beautiful thing. I am alive, and only by his grace. I live, and only by his Spirit. I lift up empty hands: I have nothing of my own to bring to God, only empty hands for him to fill.

And fill them he does, with life and life overflowing. Our Ephesians passage ends with these words: 'We are God's handiwork, created in Christ Jesus to do good works, which God prepared in advance for us to do' (2:10). Right in the centre of this verse lies again our new identity – 'in Christ Jesus' – and from this place springs the direction of our identity. We are 'God's handiwork', the Greek for 'handiwork' being *poiema*. *Poiema* is where we get our English word 'poem', and so the work God has called us to is to be, in a sense, his poems, expressions of him in the world.[5]

Paul has emphasised in Ephesians 2:1–10 that, as God's children, we are not rooted in any 'ways of this world' – standards of worth and identity provided by our culture, other people and ourselves.

We are rooted in Christ and made alive in him: we are completely loved, accepted and transformed by the grace of God. From this deep and true rootedness, we grow, a shoot extending, branches reaching out and leaves unfurling; we grow, full of God's love, and we bring God the fruit and the glory by expressing, like poetry, his love in the world. Paul prays this for the Ephesians in 3:17–19:

> I pray that you, being rooted and established in love, may have power, together with all the Lord's holy people, to grasp how wide and long and high and deep is the love of Christ, and to know this love that surpasses knowledge – that you may be filled to the measure of all the fullness of God.

God's love, as well as his power, surpasses our knowledge, Paul writes, as he prays that we may be filled to the measure of God's fullness. This is the part of the story we live when we trust in Christ and become rooted in his grace, and it is only possible through Jesus Christ making a way for us to be with God. We look at the cross, lifting our eyes to see – and we fall on to our knees, amazed, glimpsing only the edges of Jesus' love for us but knowing that it is enough.

As we come to the end of this chapter, hopefully we have glimpsed both the power and love of God in scripture, creation and history and have seen, through Paul's words, how this power and love brings us from death to life through the cross of Jesus. In the next chapter, we'll explore these big and beautiful truths through the lens of God's invitation into grace, discovering how this transforms our attitude to spending time with him – but first, join me for one last moment.

Remember Rachel, who shared Job 42 with me? A week after our first conversation, she sent me a message: 'I was praying for you and felt like I had a picture for you… I saw God stretching out his hand to you but wanting you to know that, as you take it, he won't leave you at arm's length, only holding you by the hand, but will pull you really, really close to him.'

This is the powerful, encouraging image I want to leave you with. When we open our empty hands to him, God won't leave us at arm's length – no matter what. His desire is not for us to be distant from him. Instead, as we trust in him, he'll draw us close, hold us tight and look after us with love. He longs for us to be near – how incredible is that?

Headphones time

It is good to reflect and to pray about what God is saying to us. Go somewhere quiet, with no distractions – put metaphorical headphones in your ears to block out the noise and spend time just with God. Do this however you'd like; use as many or as few of the questions below to help you.

- Think about, write down or draw a picture of what it means for God to have 'already given his all to us'.

- 'These are but the outer fringes of his works' (Job 26:14). Find a picture of the most incredible place you have ever been and reflect on the fact that it is only on the 'fringes' of God's glory. Stick the picture somewhere you'll see it, to remind you how much greater God is.

- 'Surely I spoke of things I did not understand, things too wonderful for me to know' (Job 42:3). Hold out your hands in front of you, fists clenched and facing downwards as if holding heavy shopping bags. These shopping bags are full of all the thoughts and busy things in your life. Open up your hands and drop these bags to the floor, and then turn over your hands so that your palms face upwards. Spend a few moments like this, acknowledging with God that you have empty hands before him.

- We come to God with empty hands. What beliefs or practices might you have trusted in to give you full hands or, in other words, identity and worth? How does knowing that before God we have empty hands change your view of these things?

- When we trust God, Jesus makes us alive. He fills our empty hands with grace and gives us a firm identity in him. Do you believe this? How does it make you feel, or what does it make you think? Use Ephesians 3:20–21 to pray about this and give thanks to God.

Soundtrack

'Gracefully broken' by Matt Redman (feat. Tasha Cobbs Leonard).

This song is fantastic, singing of empty-handed surrender to God who has made us his own and who is strong in our weakness. What words speak to you from this song?

The invitation

Here is a truth that heals and liberates: the One who invites you… knows you, and he knows you through and through.[6]

In the last chapter, we journeyed through the story of grace – our story, the story God has written for each of us, bringing us from death to life. This story is an invitation and a gift that calls us not only to listen and understand the story, but also to become a part of it, to draw near to God and be transformed by spending time in his life-giving presence. We are invited by God into grace; we are invited to work and walk with him and see our lives changed from the inside out, our selves renewed and restored day by day.

Read these verses from Matthew 11:28–30 (MSG):

> Are you tired? Worn out? Burned out on religion? Come to me. Get away with me and you'll recover your life. I'll show you how to take a real rest. Walk with me and work with me – watch how I do it. Learn the unforced rhythms of grace. I won't lay anything heavy or ill-fitting on you. Keep company with me and you'll learn to live freely and lightly.

This is Jesus speaking, clearly inviting you to come to him, keep company with him and grow in his grace. It's the same invitation Paul described in that Ephesians passage – the invitation from death into life, by God's grace, and the invitation to become like his poems in the world, expressions of his love to others.

Here we're going to dive even deeper, exploring more of how God's story of grace is a life-transforming invitation *into* grace. We'll question what grace really is, and we'll discover what being rooted in God's grace is all about. Take a moment to pray that God will show you more of what his grace is, that you may become rooted and established in it.

So, what actually is grace? Grab a piece of paper (or use the margin space here) and a pen; spend five minutes writing down anything that comes into your head when you think of the word 'grace'. (If you've not got a pen to hand, just take five to have a think, or you could write a list on your phone.)

I wonder what you came up with. 'Grace' is a word of brilliant mystery, containing a great depth of meaning that cannot easily be captured in a short and snappy definition. In *What's So Amazing About Grace?*, Philip Yancey explores our many, everyday uses of the word 'grace': saying grace before dinner; grace notes in music; acts of grace declared in Parliament to pardon a criminal. These uses tap into the biblical meaning of grace as something undeserved, a gift which adds flourish, beauty and life. In Yancey's words, the word 'grace' as we use it 'contains the essence of the gospels as a drop of water can contain the image of the sun'.[7] The word 'grace' captures and reflects the story of the gospel: that God has already given his all to us, undeservedly and abundantly.

I remember a definition of grace that someone once used in a children's talk at a summer camp. The speaker, in trying to explain the mystery of the word 'grace' to a group of us children, had come up with a clever acronym: grace is, he said, '**G**od's **R**escue **A**t **C**hrist's **E**xpense'.

This pithy little mnemonic stuck in my mind for years, fixing itself as a simple and easy explanation of what grace is. I hadn't realised that simplicity had come at the cost of mystery; that the concept and experience of grace had been reduced to something much smaller than it actually is.

You see, although it's definitely true that grace is ultimately expressed in the way that God rescued us through the costly death of Jesus Christ, grace is also so much greater, so much deeper, so much more present in the way that it reflects something brighter and more glorious than can be encapsulated in a memorable phrase used in a children's talk. A water droplet catches the reflection of the sun and ignites with golden light, drawing our eye to widen at the indescribable and sparkling content of sunlight. Grace catches the reflection of God's character; it ignites as it reflects the light of the world, drawing us closer to gaze at the indescribable person of Jesus Christ as his love surrounds, justifies and transforms us.

These are the three words we'll use to explore the mystery of grace: surrounding, justifying and transforming. They're all verbs; our exploration of how God invites us into grace will unfold by looking at actions of grace in the world and in our lives.

Surrounding grace

The song 'Times' by Tenth Avenue North is a beautiful expression of how ever-present grace surrounds us even in our loneliest moments. Give it a listen now, if you have a music-playing device with you.

You see, grace is everywhere: it's in the beauty and provision of creation, the serendipity of everyday life, the interactions between friends and family. It's present in art, music, sport – in everything, because it is all a free gift that has come from God's hand.

I have a friend, Nel, whose Facebook posts are a delight to read – she's a Methodist minister who posts little snippets from everyday life and ministry which are often signed off with three short words: 'All is grace'. She sometimes signs off like this even if the everyday snippet is about something tricky. Nel also hyphenates adjectives which contain '-ful': beautiful becomes 'beauty-full', delightful 'delight-full', joyful 'joy-full', and so on. This reminds me that all is indeed grace – our everyday moments, even the tricky ones, are full up of joy and grace because God is always present with us.

The surrounding nature of grace is also expressed in these words from Psalm 139:

> Where can I go from your Spirit?
>   Where can I flee from your presence?
> If I go up to the heavens, you are there;
>   if I make my bed in the depths, you are there…
> If I say, 'Surely the darkness will hide me
>   and the light become night around me,'
> even the darkness will not be dark to you;
>   the night will shine like the day,
>   for darkness is as light to you.
>
> PSALM 139:7–8, 11–12

God's grace is everywhere – his presence stretches from the highest heavens to the depths of the sea, and he is close by even in the trickiest times. God's light shines through the dark things that we find overwhelming or painful, dangerous or tempting; light touches everything that it sees with the victory of God's truth, love and grace.

Surrounding grace is therefore grace that follows us into the darkest places and turns them to light; it is grace that loved us while we were still sinners walking the wrong paths. You see, we were known and loved before the world began and we are known and loved now. God's grace awakens us to this fact by being present all around us, inviting us to see, know and love God more.

For me, the parable of the sower is another expression of surrounding grace. You'll find it in Luke 8:4–15; open your Bible (or Bible app) and give it a read.

The sower scatters the seed on every type of soil – on the path, the rock, the thorns and the good soil. The potential for roots and growth is everywhere; the sower is indiscriminate about where the seed lands. In the same way, the word of God is 'scattered' on every type of 'soil'. God doesn't discriminate about who the gospel is available to. Rather, he makes it available to all people, whether they choose to accept it or not. Jesus speaks to every person when he says, 'Come to me.' The invitation into grace is extended to all people simply by the fact that grace surrounds everyone, is present everywhere and is sown indiscriminately. The light of God refracts and bounces off every surface, awakening those who have ears to hear it to the truth and life of the gospel.

Of course, as the parable says, not everyone hears the gospel and lets it take root in their hearts. Some have the word snatched away from them; some are tempted so they lose their faith; some are choked by other distractions. Letting the word of God take root is something that takes much grace, listening and effort over time. 'Fruit is never a matter of an overnight exercise. It takes nurturing.'[8]

So, grace, by surrounding us and being ever-present, invites us to draw close to God as it awakens us to the truth of the gospel. The truth of the gospel is this: that God desires to be with his people, so much so that he takes the initiative in loving us first despite our brokenness. Surrounding grace awakens us to the brilliance of God's holiness and also to the reality of our unholiness; it shows us that we need God's grace and that we need to trust him.

Justifying grace

Grace surrounds and awakens us. Yet that is not all: grace saves and rescues us – grace *justifies* us before God, giving us what we need to be with him.

Justification is another word that contains a wealth of meaning. Paul uses it repeatedly in his letters, particularly in Galatians and Romans, to describe what we receive when we trust Jesus and his death on the cross. The Greek word translated as 'justification' can refer to both legal and religious justification: the legal justification of paying the price for one's actions, and the religious justification of being made right with God.[9] The meaning is combined in Paul: being made right with God and having a restored relationship with him involves paying the price for one's actions. It involves punishment for sin so that justice is complete and being with the holy, righteous God is possible.

We are justified not by our own actions but by Jesus' death. Paul writes in Romans 3:23 that 'all have sinned and fall short of the glory of God'. All of us, by our actions, have missed the mark when it comes to holiness; all of us have trusted our own strength. Because of that, our relationship with God is broken, beyond hope of repair by our own might. We find ourselves in need of something that will remove both death (sin's result) and temptation (sin's power).

This is why the justification we receive from Jesus is called 'grace'. Jesus did what we could not do by paying the price for our mistakes. He did this so that we could be justified and made righteous; so that we could know God and be with him. By dying, Jesus defeated death and sin and won the victory – and then gave us the victory for ourselves. In place of death, we now have life – and we have life to the full because of the grace, the free and undeserved gift, of Jesus' death. Despite missing the mark, we are made right with God through grace. Grace is the essence of the truth that we are made to be with God when once we were without him.

The invitation of justifying grace is thus: to know who we are before God and to accept Jesus as our saviour, trusting that his death and resurrection justify us and make us new. We see that surrounding grace awakens us to the closeness of God and our need for justifying grace; justifying grace invites us to become decisively rooted and established in God's love when we become awakened to our need. When we are thus rooted, we are given new life and we can be with God, and having been established each of us can say with Paul: 'I no longer live, but Christ lives in me' (Galatians 2:20).

This is the crux of identity in Jesus: we are saved by his work of grace alone. It is not by our might, nor by our strength, but totally by his grace that we come to be with God. This is a beautiful thing. Pause for a moment to reflect – you could turn to Romans 5:1–11 to think about justifying grace more, or you could revisit Ephesians 2:1–10. Take your time, I'll wait!

Transforming grace

Grace surrounds, awakens and justifies us in God's sight. Grace brings us from death to life – yet it does not stop there! Grace takes us and transforms us from the inside out, changing us so that we no longer behave like those 'deserving of wrath' (to use the phrase from Ephesians 2), but instead become God's holy poetry, expressions of his love in the world.

1 Peter 1:14–16 says this:

> As obedient children, do not conform to the evil desires you had when you lived in ignorance. But just as he who called you is holy, so be holy in all you do; for it is written: 'Be holy because I am holy.'

Be holy, Peter exhorts. God has made you his own through his grace that justifies – take on his likeness because he is your Father and you are his children. Be obedient to him and grow in holiness, because holy and good is what you are made to be.

Transforming grace is grace that purifies and cleanses us. It's grace that, to use a biblical word, *sanctifies* us – grace that makes us holy. It's grace that shapes us so that we reflect our established identity in Christ. Peter is saying that, because God has already justified us, so we should learn to live out our new identity in Jesus, becoming holy in all that we do. Grace doesn't just leave us where it found us; it continually transforms us so that we become more Christlike in how we act, think and speak. Grace transforms us from the inside out, surrounding us always, to help us.

But how does this transformation happen? Does change take place when we try harder, or when we demand that God does this or that to make us into better people? Are we sanctified when we make lists of rules to follow (and inevitably forget to follow them)? I think not!

Transformation happens when we are close to Jesus. Remember the invitation from Matthew 11? Jesus calls to us to keep company with him because it is only in his presence that we 'learn the unforced rhythms of grace'. Grace transforms us in the context of freedom and relationship rather than pressure and demand: Jesus' burden is light, his workload easy and his voice gentle and encouraging while also challenging.

Think back to the parable of the sower. We saw that transformation happens over a period of time; plants need to be nurtured in order for fruit to grow. It is the same with us – transformation takes time and nurturing. To be made holy as our Father is holy, we need to be patient with God and ourselves, trusting that God's timing is perfect and that our effort will be honoured by him.

It's so important to remember that 'grace is not opposed to effort. It is opposed to earning. Effort is action. Earning is attitude.'[10] We must throw off the attitude of earning our worth when we accept God's gift of grace – yet we must not forget to keep putting effort into striving for holiness. Grace spurs us on to act, causing us to run forwards in the path of God's commands. This is because God doesn't transform us while we sit passively by and watch – he invites us into the middle of the work of transformation, calling us to be committed to sending down roots by the streams so that we may grow tall and strong and bear good fruit.

This is exciting! It's an invitation to partner with *God himself* as he builds his kingdom in our midst. It is an invitation to 'work out your salvation… for it is God who works in you to will and to act in order to fulfil his good purpose' (Philippians 2:12–13).

Despite the joy I feel as I write these words, I must say that they are not words that I have come by easily. These are words and truths that I have learned over time as I've walked and worked with God – in the late-night hours of scribbling down everything that doesn't make sense; in the empty-handed prayers as I've prepared for the day; in the challenging words of sermons, conversations and Bible reading. Coming to know God more deeply, learning to grow deeper roots in his grace, takes time and effort (and often mistakes); being transformed from the inside out takes wrestling and repetition until you've got it.

It's only when I've paused and looked back over a period of time and realised that I am not the same as I was a year ago, three years ago, five years ago, that I have seen that God has been transforming and renewing me day by day. It's in retrospect that you see how God has brought fruit from your life; it's as you look back that you see the messiness of present moments spiralling out to shine with the brilliant light of God's glory. In the present moment, growing roots in God's grace often looks and feels a lot harder and more confusing than you ever expect it to be. But it's so worth it. God's word never comes back empty (Isaiah 55:11).

The rest of this book will get stuck into this messy, exciting, everyday pursuit of walking with Jesus and learning to dwell in his grace by exploring some 'means of grace',[11] some spiritual disciplines or practices that help us to know God. Richard Foster uses the term 'disciplined grace' to talk about the work and walk of being transformed by grace: to get to the place where God can transform us, we must walk 'the path of disciplined grace' into his presence. He writes:

> It is 'grace' because it is free; it is 'disciplined' because there is something for us to do. In *The Cost of Discipleship*, Dietrich

> Bonhoeffer makes it clear that grace is free, but it is not cheap. The grace of God is unearned and unearnable, but if we ever expect to grow in grace, we must pay the price of a consciously chosen course of action which involves both individual and group life.[12]

It is clear that grace is free, unearned and undeserved. Yet it is not 'cheap'. We do not grow in grace by sitting still. We must keep step with Jesus and consciously choose to walk the path of 'disciplined grace', for this is how we accept the invitation to grow roots in God's grace. This is how we come to bear fruit to his glory and others' benefit.

The 'disciplines' that Foster refers to are things that you may be familiar with already: prayer, Bible reading, meditation, fasting, going to church, pilgrimage and service are just a few of the ways that we can walk with Jesus and deepen our roots in his grace. In the rest of this book, we will explore a couple of general ideas related to disciplines of faith, or 'rhythms of rootedness' as I have called them: the value of habit, and how to persevere even when it's hard – before focusing on a specific few practices: Bible study, private prayer, enjoying creation, entering into silence, church services or liturgy and church community.

I write about these rhythms from a perspective of experiences and stories of what has most helped me over the past years, not from a place of having studied an exhaustive list and doctrine of different disciplines. If you're looking for something that discusses the latter, I hope that you explore other reading and resources (some of which you will find in the 'Recommendations' section on page 150) about disciplines and rhythms that I don't mention.

Aside from this, I have just one last point I want to raise before we embark of the adventure of exploring rhythms of rootedness. It is this: we don't accept the invitation of grace alone and we don't walk the path of disciplined grace by ourselves. We walk *with* Jesus. It's the beauty of 'with' once more, and the beauty of the words Rachel sent to me: as you take God's hand, he won't leave you at arm's length but he will draw you really, really close to him. He will help you to grow those roots in his grace – it's not by our power or by our strength, but by his grace that we grow in his grace. Grace surrounds us in this pursuit, too.

On summer break from university, I journeyed to a little monastery in Assisi in Italy with some people from my college. We stayed there for one week on retreat: five days to rest and pray, soak up the sun, help to tame the monastery's vineyards and visit the beautiful churches (and ice cream shops!) of Assisi. On the first day, I was asked to read the reflective English reading in the midday prayer service (everything else was said or sung in Italian). The reading was from Isaac of Nineveh's *The Ascetical Treatises* and it was all about God's Spirit helping us to pray. This is it:

> When the Spirit dwells within a person, from the moment that person has become prayer, the Spirit never leaves them. For the Spirit himself never ceases to pray within us. Whether we are asleep or awake, from then on prayer never departs from our soul. Whether we are eating or drinking or sleeping or whatever else we may be doing, even if we are in the deepest of sleeps, the incense of prayer is rising without effort in our heart. Prayer never again deserts us. In every moment of our life, even when it appears to have ceased, prayer is secretly at work within us continuously.[13]

I love these words. Stop. Read them again. Let them sink in.

As God's children, we have God's Spirit in our hearts, with us – and the Spirit is continuously praying from within us, continually crying out to God even when we feel distant from him. Galatians 4:6 is a stunning verse: 'Because you are his sons, God sent the Spirit of his Son into our hearts, the Spirit that cries out "*Abba*, Father".'

What more confirmation can there be that we are completely, firmly and forever rooted and established in God's love? What more do we need to help us grow deeper roots? We have the Spirit of God himself, God-with-us, crying out from our hearts! This is the greatest encouragement and it is a grace upon grace already given: not only are we made to be with God even when we did not deserve it, but we are helped in our continual walking with God, from now into eternity. We have much to celebrate, much to give thanks for.

Romans 8:26 speaks about the Spirit helping us as well: 'The Spirit helps us in our weakness. We do not know what we ought to pray for, but the Spirit himself intercedes for us through wordless groans.' I experienced this in Madrid when I was on a challenge called 'Escape and Pray', run by the student Christian charity Fusion.[14] I signed up with three friends, Holly, Miriam and Flora. Fusion booked us plane tickets to an unknown destination. We turned up at the airport at 6.00 am on a Friday and opened an orange envelope to find out where we were going. We had 48 hours in that location to pray for churches and student groups, as part of Fusion's vision to encourage students in faith and build up a network of 10,000 student-friendly churches across Europe.

My friends and I sat on the plane to Madrid with only €20 each, nowhere to stay that evening and hardly any contacts in Spain. We were understandably nervous – and this is where God came in. Throughout the 48 hours, God provided for and encouraged us in ways that were immeasurably more than we could ask or imagine. One of these ways was by reminding us of Romans 8, both throughout the weekend and before it, with that verse about the Spirit helping us to pray right at the centre. Even when we were hot, tired out and wanting to go home, God's Spirit gave us direction about where to go, who to speak to and what to pray – even if that prayer was a wordless cry from our hearts.

Keeping company with Jesus is adventurous, fun and always surprising. I never expected to be standing in the Puerta del Sol in central Madrid watching my friends preach to passers-by from a Red Box;[15] I never thought that I would be writing a second book to encourage people in their faith. I never imagined that I'd have the confidence to stand up and speak to a group of people – and now, I find myself giving talks at youth groups and summer camp.

This sounds like I'm boasting in what I've done – but I'm really not. I'm boasting in the grace of Christ which has worked in me and through me to make me what I am. I still get it wrong more often than I get it right; I still forget or ignore God; I still get nervous, stressed and worn out by life; I still get cross and frustrated with myself and with other people. Yet I can always rely on Jesus' transforming grace and his Spirit residing with me as I walk that path of disciplined grace with him, that path of both free gift and effort, of God working in me as I work out my salvation. He draws me close and from that relationship there is fruit, fruit that surprises me even as it brings glory to God.

Because this is what it is all about: growing our roots in God's grace so that fruit might spring up to bring God's kingdom near. It's about noticing where God's surrounding grace is and drawing closer to him through practices of prayer, Bible and church, and it's about partnering with God's grace to see something new come to life in your life and in the lives of those around you. You'll be amazed at what starts to happen as you start to pray.

I will leave you here with a verse to encourage you. It's a vision of the renewal God desires to bring about through his people that seek him: 'See, I am doing a new thing!' the voice of God declares in Isaiah 43:19. 'Now it springs up; do you not perceive it? I am making a way in the wilderness and streams in the wasteland.' I am bringing new life from dust; from roots in my grace I will bring fruit.

Headphones time

This has been a full-on chapter, packed with theology and stories. Think and pray through everything you've read – use the questions below, or simply ask God to speak.

- What have you encountered here that is new to you? How has it challenged and/or encouraged you in your walk with God?

- The word 'invitation' has appeared several times in this chapter. To reflect on God's invitation into grace, get some paper and pens and write an invitation from Jesus to you using the words of Matthew 11:28–30. Keep the invitation somewhere you'll see it so that you'll be reminded of how God has invited you to walk with him.

- In *Ten Thousand Gifts*, Ann Voskamp writes about a challenge she once took to write a list of 1,000 everyday gifts from God that she could give thanks for. You could try this yourself – grab a notebook to keep with you, and jot down anything that you are thankful to God for.

- Have you ever looked back on your life and realised that God has transformed and grown you in ways that you didn't realise at the time? If not, why don't you do that now? Ask God to show you how his grace has been working in you, and write down both the challenges and encouragements from that reflection.

- Graham Beynon writes about the fruit of the Spirit (in Galatians 5:22–23) that 'this is a character we keep on growing in. The fruit continues to develop and we can never say, "We're done".'[16] What do you think of this? Does it make you excited that a life spent with Jesus is a life of continually growing in grace? Why, or why not?

Soundtrack

'Whatever you're doing' by Sanctus Real.

A friend sent this song to me when I was in the middle of a chaotic time when I couldn't quite see how God's grace was bringing fruit. It helped me to keep trusting that God was making all things new and healing the things that hurt. What does it say to you about grace?

SECTION II
Rhythms of rootedness

3

Becoming rooted day by day

The value of habits and rhythms

Habits are to the soul what veins are to the blood. The very course of our life depends on them. Random acts of greatness pale in comparison to habitual acts of faithfulness.[17]

A few years ago, the third sentence of the above quotation was posted on Facebook as a phone wallpaper. I downloaded the picture and set it as my phone's background. For the following months, I saw the words every time I logged into my phone to check emails, scroll through social media, take a photo, send a text. It became a sentence that shaped and moulded my prayers and the rest of my life; it was something that, through repetition, became a lens through which I viewed the world and my actions. 'Random acts of greatness pale in comparison to habitual acts of faithfulness': it's the everyday, faithful habits that God desires of me, not the flashy, one-off displays of greatness that are so often mistaken for true faith.

What are the habits that make up your life? We all have them, those little routines and rhythms that guide us through the days, weeks, months and years. We mark our hours by those practices that we return to again and again: the first-thing-in-the-morning coffee to wake you up; the post-church visit to the supermarket to buy the week's food; the monthly meeting with your teacher, supervisor or boss; the Christmas pause at the end of every year.

We are formed by the habits that we adopt; our repeated actions become who we are by directing what our minds and hands are occupied by. This is why I wanted to include a chapter dedicated entirely to exploring the value of habit – because it is indeed incredibly valuable, and can become a useful tool for growing roots in God's grace.

In her book *God Hunting*, Jo Swinney includes an interview with Pete Greig, founder and director of the 24–7 prayer movement. They chat about prayer, touching on both its difficulties and joys. Greig says this:

> I think that one of the keys for me is to try and see prayer as something embedded in normality and not removed from it. There's a lovely old Celtic prayer that says, 'I make this bed in the name of the Father, the Son and the Holy Spirit.'[18]

Knowing God is something that should be embedded in our 'everyday, ordinary life – [our] sleeping, eating, going-to-work, and walking-around life' (Romans 12:1, MSG). It shouldn't be cloistered away and kept separate from our everyday rhythms and routines. Rather, we experience prayer and spending time with God at their fullest when they become the key rhythms and patterns of our normal lives, actions that we continually return to and habits that form and influence who we are.

It's about letting our identity and trust in God shape how we live our whole lives, teaching us to seek his kingdom first, through and before everything else that we do. One really practical example is that of a 'breath prayer', a very short prayer you pray with every breath. The prayer could be a name of God, like 'Abba' or 'good shepherd', or it could be a simple phrase like 'Come, Lord Jesus'. One person writes:

> I've been using the same breath prayer for a couple of years now. It is said that over time, the prayer becomes a river flowing beneath your consciousness – I've found that to be true. Now when I'm not focused on something else, what's the first thing that pops into my mind? Come, Lord Jesus! It feels like the

synapses of my brain have been rerouted, through repetition, towards invoking the presence of God.[19]

Try this for yourself: choose a short phrase you could use as a breath prayer, and call it to mind in every spare moment.

Another simple way that you could seek God through the day is by praying when you clean your teeth (seriously). When you brush your top teeth, give thanks to God; when you brush your bottom teeth, pray about the day or night ahead.

How about writing a Bible verse on your mirror or setting one as your phone background, so that every time you look at your mirror or phone you're reminded of God's truth? What about writing little notes about God's love and grace on future days in your diary, so that when you come to those days you see words about God? Try to say grace every time you eat – whether you say it out loud or in your head, it's a really simple way of reminding you to give thanks to God. Maybe extend your walk to university, school or work so that you can spend a few moments asking God to show you his love before you get to where you're going. It's so practical and simple: embed prayer in normality by finding little ways to tie spending time with God to your everyday routines and habits. Jot down some ideas now: they can be as crazy as praying while you clean your teeth or as simple as the breath prayer; get creative in how you seek his kingdom first!

To return to the interview in *God Hunting*, Greig also says that 'it is important to carve intentional time out so that you can recentre on Jesus and live the rest of your life more aware of his presence'.[20] It's not just about doing the little, everyday things tied to the habits you already have; it's also about committing significant chunks of time to spend with Jesus, without distractions. Carve out the time; commit to those more intentional spaces of recentring your life on him. From this springs the rest of your living – you'll find that everyday habits of seeking him become easier when you first make space for those carved-out times of prayer.

It's a bit like exercising. We set aside specific times within our everyday lives to exercise. In those intentional, carved-out times we build up our muscles and get our hearts working. We then experience the benefits even in the times when we're not exercising: we enjoy healthier, happier bodies in our everyday lives.

Similarly, in the specific, carved-out, intentional time we spend with God, we strengthen our spiritual muscles and get our hearts beating in time with his. In the times inbetween, we enjoy a greater awareness of his presence, developed and built up by our time spent listening closely to his voice.

Paul uses similar imagery in his first letter to the Corinthians (9:24–27):

> Do you not know that in a race all the runners run, but only one gets the prize? Run in such a way as to get the prize. Everyone who competes in the games[21] goes into strict training. They do it to get a crown that will not last; but we do it to get a crown that will last for ever. Therefore, I do not run like someone running aimlessly; I do not fight like a boxer beating the air. No, I strike a blow to my body and make it my slave so that after I have preached to others, I myself will not be disqualified for the prize.

The metaphor of competitive running is used to explain to the Corinthians the kind of life God calls them to lead – a life of intentionality, effort and perseverance. Living the life God has called you to is like learning to run well in a race: to win the prize, you have to strive forwards and train hard, cultivating your body so that you can run with purpose. You have to build up the muscles that will carry you to claim the crown that will last for ever, becoming the person God wants you to be as you work out your salvation while he works in you.

This intentional, carved-out time of 'training' and spending time with Jesus can look different for each person. Some might study a bit of the Bible each day; others might sit in silence and listen for God's voice. It could involve worship music, creative prayer or more formal patterns of prayer – one person might spend time with Jesus while walking; another might need to be in a really quiet place. The one key thing is that it is *regular*. Growing in grace happens through *habitual, regular acts of faithfulness*, not one-off moments of greatness.

Let's define 'faithfulness'. When we think of faith or belief, we often think of mental assent to a set of facts or truths. Faith becomes about what we believe – whether or not we ascribe to defined sets of doctrines. Yet, while faith does involve believing the facts of the gospel, it is much more about *how we live because of the gospel* rather than what we believe *about* it. Faith is active, not passive. When we read verses such as Mark 1:15, in which Jesus says, 'The kingdom of God has come near. Repent and believe the good news!', we should read 'believe' with the sense of actively *trusting*, actually *stepping out* in faith and *living* in the way that Jesus has called us to.

Alan Hargrave writes in *One For Sorrow*:

> I think Christians, for far too long and even now, have focused unhelpfully on what we say we believe… For the most part, Jesus defines discipleship by trust in him and by what we do, rather than what we say we believe. Indeed, the very word 'faith' does not refer to a set of metaphysical propositions which I may, or may not, sign up to. Rather it means something more like 'risky faithfulness'. It is about how you live it out.[22]

Faithfulness: it's risky and adventurous, *lived* more than thought about. Habitual acts of faithfulness transform us, taking us on God's path of deeply exciting and subversive new life – taking us to see him make all things new.

This doesn't mean that it's easy, this *lived* faith. It takes effort and perseverance: 'Our lives do need to be cultivated in order to make them a context in which faith can flourish – soil in which God's word will grow strong and bear fruit.'[23]

Let's look at three challenges and encouragements to take with us as we go.

1 Just like seeds that grow slowly, putting down their roots in the unseen underground, so our growth in God's grace develops slowly in the unseen places

My wonderful friend Emma wrote a blog post called 'Control'. It popped up in my newsfeed; I clicked on it and became immediately engrossed in reading her words. They were words which told the story of Emma's struggle with being in control, a struggle which played out in school projects, exams, and issues of food and body image.[24]

She writes about the process of learning to trust God:

> For me, learning to trust in God and hand over the steering wheel to him has been a slow and gradual process… Trust in God doesn't just happen with a click of the fingers; it starts with the recognition that our ways are flawed and utterly, utterly rubbish when you compare them to the plans of the One who created the whole earth. It involves promising every morning that you will try to follow His way and not your own… Once I started… it became easier, and it spread throughout the rest of my life.[25]

The journey of prayer and reflection that Emma has taken through the last few years has been 'slow and gradual', happening over a long period of time – like a plant that bears its first fruit after three or four years. It's involved committing to put God's way first at the start of every day. From that place of habitually refocusing on God, Emma found that the trust she learned from dwelling in God's presence 'spread throughout the rest of [her] life'.

When we commit to habits of faithfully dwelling with God, the lessons we learn with him slowly overflow into the rest of our lives. God transforms us through the times we spend with him, even if we don't immediately see the results, and even if others don't know about the process that's going on between you and God until it finally emerges out into the open. The roots of some plants grow for a long while underground before we ever see any leaves overground – this can be the case as we grow in grace. As we develop habits of faithfulness, we must be patient and wait, and work as we go. God will bring fruit precisely when he means to.

2 Just as plants go through different seasons of growth throughout the year, so do our patterns of growth change with different 'seasons' in our lives

When I was at school, rhythms of spending time with God felt easier in some ways. This was because each day was more structured: I had a consistent pattern to follow five out of seven days in the week. Now I'm at university, this is not the case! Every day is different, with so many choices to make about when I should study, sleep and socialise. My time is my own and it's therefore a lot more flexible; this makes it a little trickier to establish consistent patterns of prayer.

And this is okay! Just as plants develop differently in winter than they do in summer or autumn or spring, so we can grow in different ways. The rhythms we adopt depend on the changes we're going through and the circumstances we find ourselves in. Building up habits of spending time with God is not about deciding one day that for the rest of your life you are going to pray for one hour from 8.00– 9.00 am every morning; although this might work for one stage of your life, it might not work for another.

Rather, developing helpful habits of prayer requires sensitivity to the rest of our lives as well. For example, you might want to commit to the habit of reading a chapter of the Bible every day. The question is: when would be the best time to do this? Is it practical for you to read it as soon as you get up, or will you have more time and energy to focus if you read it over your lunch break or in the evening before you sleep? The 'season' you're in might affect *how* you read the Bible as well: are you going through a really busy time that means that you just need to read the Bible simply, letting the words wash over you? Or do you need to wrestle with a particular issue a bit more, meaning that you might want to read a Bible commentary or study guide alongside each day's chapter as well?

Working at building up habits of faithfulness becomes easier when you're sensitive to your whole life. It's not about setting a high standard to achieve – it's about working out what would be the most helpful way for you to carve out time to spend with God. Listen to God as you decide what habits to adopt and pursue: his burden is easy and his workload light, and he loves and knows you completely. He knows exactly how, when and where would be best for you to spend intentional time with him; follow his lead freely.

3 Just as small seeds grow into tall trees, so does our faith grow when we keep company with Jesus

I love the parable of the mustard seed (Mark 4:30–32):

> Again he said, 'What shall we say the kingdom of God is like, or what parable shall we use to describe it? It is like a mustard seed, which is the smallest of all seeds on earth. Yet when planted, it grows and becomes the largest of all garden plants, with such big branches that the birds can perch in its shade.'

Every summer, I help on an 8–11-year-olds' summer camp. One year, we had an evening meeting that was all about the mustard seed parable. I listened to some other leaders give the talk and, despite it being short, simple and aimed at children, I was completely blown away. 'God takes something tiny and grows it into something big and beautiful,' I wrote later. 'He takes our offerings, however small and not good enough, and brings them to fruit. His kingdom is built on the small things we bring – the mustard seeds.'

Mustard seeds are absolutely tiny – yet when they grow, they are wild and untameable; they continually drop more and more seeds so that you can never get rid of the plant. Our small, persevering efforts of growing in faithfulness are like this, wildly and irrevocably bringing the kingdom of God in our midst. So, when you're starting to develop habits and rhythms of dwelling with God, be encouraged that small starts are good, and that God takes our small beginnings to build his kingdom and bring his light into the world. As a character from Tolkien's Middle Earth says: some believe 'that it is only great power that can hold evil in check, but that is not what I have found. I have found it is the small things, everyday deeds of ordinary folk, that keeps darkness at bay.'[26]

So be encouraged, and be challenged. As we journey through the rest of this book, ask yourself this question: what habits is God asking me to work at? How can I embed prayer in normality and carve out time to spend with Jesus?

Headphones time

Pause and pray – pray for God to show you the habits of faithfulness that he wants to help you grow in. Use the questions below if that helps!

- Have you ever thought about prayer as something to be embedded in normality? Choose and commit to trying one of the ideas you jotted down about how this could work in your life.

- 'We are not called to be perfectly awesome. We are called to be imperfectly faithful, because we have been perfectly loved, liberated and highly esteemed by the Most High.'[27] How does knowing that God loves and liberates you encourage and challenge you as you think about habits of spending time with him? Read and pray through Psalm 139 – God knows and loves you this much!

- What stops you from carving out intentional time to spend with God? How can you start to overcome some of these challenges?

- Find some mustard seeds and hold them in your hand. Reflect on how the smallness of our acts of faithfulness can bring fruit for God's kingdom when his grace helps us to grow. Pray for his grace to guide you as you keep company with Jesus and learn from him.

- Does the definition of faith and faithfulness explored above change how you've thought about faith up until now? If so, how? If not, how can you continue to put this definition into practice in your life?

Soundtrack

'The garden' by Kari Jobe.

This song speaks to me about the faithfulness of God and the promise of renewal his love brings. How does it encourage you to adopt habits of following him?

Story stop: Leaves

This is the first of the story stops, a little moment to pause and read a childhood story of mine that's helped me to think about how I can be rooted in God's grace. Have a read of the story and short reflection at the end, and maybe spend some time thinking about your own experiences and how they've helped you to know God better.

The child's hazel eyes blinked up at the crisp autumn sky, vastly visible from the perspective of a pushchair. The child was perhaps two; this was one of her first autumns. Her mum pushed her along a gravel path, the wheels of the pushchair making a sound like Velcro as they ground over the tiny stones. The little girl loved this sound and grinned, eyes blinking in the light.

Suddenly, a blurry orange shape came into view, twirling and swirling from somewhere high up. Her grin became a look of puzzlement as more orange shapes appeared and floated down – look! There was one there, and there – and even over there by the gate into the park. A breeze whooshed across the path; an orange shape drifted right into her lap.

She touched it curiously. It was thin, and the edges crumbled to tiny, dusty pieces as her fingertips closed around them. It had a stalk and little lines all over it, and it looked familiar despite being utterly strange. It reminded her of leaves, big green leaves on the trees. She lifted up the shape above her head: 'Mummy, what is it?'

Her mum stopped and came round to the front of the pushchair. 'It's a leaf, Hannah, from the trees,' she said, pointing up at the tall trunks and high branches around them.

The girl, Hannah (or, in other words, me), looked up to the trees... and there was nothing green there! I looked back at my mum, shocked.

'When it gets to autumn, after summer, the leaves go orange and brown and fall off the trees. They land on the ground – look, there's one falling now!' My mum pointed to another leaf spiralling down. I looked and promptly started to cry.

'Why? Stick leaves back on?' It was sad that the leaves fell off the branches; leaves belong on trees and trees look lonely and sad without them. Surely the leaves could be stuck back on? The trees didn't have to be sad forever.

Mum laughed and explained. 'It's okay, Hannah. The leaves have to fall off so that new ones can grow. If they didn't fall off there wouldn't be room for new, big green leaves in the springtime – they have to fall off. These orange leaves look pretty too, don't they? And wouldn't it be sad if the new ones had no space to grow?'

My mum has often told this story to me. I don't really remember it, so this has been written with imagination's help – yet I have found it a really useful (and amusing) little tale to think about.

I cried when the leaves fell off the trees, thinking that it was wrong and that the trees were sad and lost without their big green leaves. Yet it was actually right and good that the leaves crinkled up, turned brown and fell to the ground. The leaves had to fall so that new life could grow; the old had to go so that the new could come.

How does this connect with your thinking about habitual acts of faithfulness? Ask God to show you the old habits you're finding it hard to let go of and the new habits he wants to establish in your life.

Honey from the rock

Walking in faith even when it's hard

**But you would be fed with the finest of wheat;
with honey from the rock I would satisfy you.**
PSALM 81:16

So, you've thought about habits: the habits you have now and the ones you might like to adopt to help you grow in God's grace. You might have thought about your past experiences of trying to build up such rhythms – if not, have a think now.

As you look back, notice the times when you've seen lots of growth and it's been fun to stick to your habits of faithfulness. You've kept company with Jesus by returning to him every day, and you've seen God's grace transform your life. God has helped you overcome fear and become more confident in who you are. He's taken a situation or a relationship that's been really messy, and in the place of brokenness he's brought resolution and peace. Perhaps he's used you – your willingness, creativity and prayers – to bring a friend to Jesus. Look back and remember how you felt in the middle of these times: strong and rooted, smiling up at God as he shows you the fruit he's bringing.

Yet, as you continue to look back over your walk and work with Jesus, you will not only see times of clearly abundant grace and light. You will also see times where you've been stumbling around in the dark, wondering how the pain or conflict will ever end; when God will hear your prayers; how you'll deal with the grief and the anger; what the fruit is that God is bringing from your life, if he's bringing any at all. You've experienced struggle and wrestling, sitting in the midnight hours with no energy left to cry and the weight of the world pressing on your shoulders. You weren't able in these times to ignore the heap of seemingly insurmountable problems looming large next to you – temptations and unholy habits were loud in their stubbornness; situations beyond your control made you lose hope; loss and heartache marked you with deep, seemingly incurable wounds. Look back on those times and remember how you felt in the depths of them: weak, clinging to God's grace by your fingernails, weathering the storm by gritting your teeth and hoping your roots will stay somehow in the soil.

This is what life is like: light and dark, joyful and painful. One grieving father writes: 'Lament and love. That about sums up my existence.'[28] It's a life of tensions and opposites – and that's okay, because God is there in the tensions, somehow. He's there both as you stand open-armed on the mountaintop and when you're completely shattered on the valley floor, unable to move. When we seek God in the hard places – even if to seek him is to shout angrily at him – we find him. We find him as we faithfully persevere in listening to him, seeking him and obeying him (no matter how hard this is). As we trust Jesus and fall into the palm of God's hand, even when we can't see where his hand is taking us, we find God. We find his incomparable and indescribable character that always tends towards life, that always gives us what we need to grow. Our roots grow deep in his grace even in our crippling weaknesses, because God is strong for us even when we are weak. He loves us.

One of my own stories of experiencing this comes from the time I mentioned in the first chapter: the first term of my second university year, where everything felt like a desert and a dark place. At the time, I didn't really know why I was struggling so much; I only knew that I felt like Elijah heading out into the wilderness for a long 40 days. Sitting with those feelings was hard and walking through them was harder – here, I'll tell you the tales of some key moments in that journey by weaving them together into one story, the story of a walk home.[29]

I walk through the tall metal gates, stepping from the muddy path of the Cambridge backs on to the smoother walkway of Clare College's avenue. The air's November-cold; my breath clouds out in front of me as my bag strap cuts into my shoulder with the weight of too many library books. I'm tired; I just want to get home, get warm and get some food. I look up at the bare pale branches laced above me, a fragile canopy illuminated by greenish lamps shining against the darkening sky. I try to ignore the thoughts circling in my head, but they're thoughts that have been circling for a while, feelings that I've been ignoring that just won't go away.

I think back to a few months before. I'd sat among the Jesus Green wildflowers and considered their beauty and fragility, and I'd written these words:

> I've been learning out of a place of often feeling empty and a little bit unseeing, a place that is hard to describe. A bit of a wilderness perhaps… however hard I try, I can't make sense of everything: I can't see or control or fix or understand how the whole of this life is unfolding. I can't sustain myself or keep my feet walking the dusty path by my own strength. Prayer is hard.

This matter has come to a head in these last three words. Prayer is hard: speaking to my Father and hearing from him has become hard. God's voice is too obscure and distant – or I am not good enough to hear it – or he is just not speaking in the way I want him to. I am tying myself up in knots and, as I cross the curved arch of Clare bridge on that cold evening with my library books, the knots feel too tight and my own strength too fragile for me even to want to acknowledge them.

At the bridge's centre, I stop, leaning out between two stony spheres to gaze towards King's College. The evening light is blue and not yet starry. My shoulder feels the relief when I shove my bag to the floor; I breathe out and wordlessly pray from that empty place, that place of knots.

I watch for stars and remember the first morning at my new church. I'd started crying (which is really out of character for me) and I didn't quite know why. A friend I barely knew put her arm around me and prayed these incredibly relevant words: 'Blessed is the one who has not seen, but yet believed.'

'Blessed is the one who has not seen, but yet believed': Jesus spoke these words to Thomas who doubted, Thomas who wouldn't believe until he'd put his hands in the resurrected Jesus' wounds. Thomas perplexedly couldn't see or understand what had happened – and so he didn't believe. Jesus invites us to believe even though we cannot always see his plans and purposes; even when we feel tied up in knots. Even when we struggle to persevere faithfully with God because we cannot see the fruit of it, he calls us to believe. And those who believe he calls 'blessed'.

I haul up my bag and head away from the bridge. Five minutes later, I turn from Trinity Lane on to King's Parade; I stop again as I spot the lights on in one of the art shops. In the window, I see a woman preparing canvases to be painted or wrapped or displayed or *something* – and I realise that God similarly prepares us. We may not know why or what for, and our experiences of struggle may speak against our hope that something good is happening or will happen again. But even when we cannot see, we can still believe. We can still be blessed. God is still good, and he still has good things for us to do, both in the unseeing wilderness and after it.

I turn away and turn my headphones up loud. A favourite song comes on and, as I walk, my thoughts turn to the lyrics and the sound rather than prayer and perplexity. The song shuffles to another as

I turn on to Bridge Street – and see with new eyes something which had been there for a while but which I hadn't yet noticed. A string of bright Christmas lights – red, green, blue, yellow, white – mark the way from Magdalene Bridge to where Bridge Street crosses with Chesterton Lane, my street.

The lights sparkle like promises: there are lights in this wilderness.

The dark places in our lives, the places of yearning for restoration, refreshment, renewal and new life – these places where our need is great and our weakness greater – these are the places that show up God's light.

Just like fairy lights along my path home and like Christmas lights along the path of Advent (that season of precious waiting, anticipating and hoping), so God's promises are. The promises of his faithfulness, goodness and forever-love shine like coloured lights, each bulb illuminating the next little bit of the path through the darkness. They might not reveal the whole distance all at once, but they do give us enough light to take the next few steps forwards. God gives us the light to walk in his light even through dark places: for even darkness is as light to him (Psalm 139:11–12).

I follow the coloured lights to their end, turn on to Chesterton Lane and fall into the warmth of my house. I drop my bag, wriggle out of my big coat and boots, and head to the kitchen to cook up some food. There's light even in darkness; God is our strength even when we're fragile and unseeing. I remind myself of this grace – and pray that it writes itself on my heart.

These moments and truths from that term strengthened me in ways that I'm still discovering. It's a journey ongoing; we walk with God from now until forever, and along the way we find treasure that's immeasurably more than we could ask or imagine – even in seasons of lament and numbness. We adventure to places we didn't think we'd ever go, and all the while God reminds us that our roots are in him no matter what routes we take. Whatever messy darknesses we encounter and whatever wilderness places God takes us to, we can be sure that he is with us. We can be sure that persevering and keeping with that habitual attitude of seeking him is totally worth it, for he *always* brings fruit even when we cannot see it.

He always brings 'honey from the rock', as Psalm 81:16 puts it. I first heard this phrase in Assisi, in Italian: *miele dalla roccia*. Something stirred when I heard those foreign words; later I looked them up and they amazed me. They appear at the end of a psalm of reminding and warning – have a read of it now (Psalm 81).

The psalm begins with praise: God rescued his people when they called out to him – bring out your music; sing loud songs, for we have much to celebrate!

The mood turns in verse 8: 'Hear me, my people,' calls God, 'and I will warn you.' Although I rescued you, you have forgotten me. Turn back; I long to be your God! 'Open wide your mouth and I will fill it,' God promises.

This makes me think of baby birds opening their tiny, fragile beaks surprisingly wide so that their parent bird can feed them. It's a picture of utter dependency and trust. God invites his people to open wide their mouths so that he can feed them; he longs for his people to fully rely on him, even in adversity, so that he can satisfy their needs. He will satisfy them with all that they need: 'But you would be fed with the finest of wheat; with honey from the rock I would satisfy you.' God will give his people 'the finest of wheat' and 'honey from the rock', both beautifully luxurious foods. Even more – that sweet, luxurious, delightful honey is *from the rock*: from the hard place, the unexpected and difficult place.

For us, the hard place could be any of the struggles we've mentioned before: feeling like it's hard to pray; being in the middle of a messy relationship or situation; getting hurt by any manner of tragedy, loss, illness or stress. You would not expect to find honey there, but God does the unexpected thing and brings honey from the rock, sustaining and feeding you even in your darkest night.

Hear this, because you're not alone: we all bear marks of brokenness. We all have wounds. We all journey at times through wilderness places of rocks and doubt, whether we understand them or not. We all cry out to God and ask him *why* and *how long*, and we often don't receive the answers we expect.

Yet, no matter what, we all also receive this one amazing thing: honey from the rock. Sweetness in the midst of bitterness. Beauty in the midst of pain. New life sprouting from dead branches. Abundance pouring out over the places where we once had deep wounds.

There's light in your darkness, and it's God's light, somewhere and somehow. There's honey coming out from the rock, and it's by God's gracious, loving hand that this happens. In the midst of your tricky time, return to those habits of seeking him: open wide your mouth for, surely, he will fill it.

Take confidence in this. Because God's light shines through darkness and because his honey comes from the rock, you can boldly go wherever darkness needs to be overcome.[30] You can be bold in your praying and in your seeking of God's kingdom, because you know that God's abundance comes in the midst of any trial. And you can give thanks in all circumstances, too: 'When life is sweet, say thank you and celebrate. And when life is bitter, say thank you and grow.'[31]

From brokenness can come abundance. 'Wounds are what break open the soul to plant the seeds of a deeper growth.'[32] These words are stunning in their challenge to see that God really does work everything for the good of those who love him (Romans 8:28–39). Don't get me wrong, I am not saying that suffering and hurt are God's intention. Not at all. The cause for suffering isn't God's desire or will.

While we have no answers to the mystery of suffering and hard times, we can ask a new question: what, in this darkness that I don't understand, is God showing me about himself? How is he turning this situation around for his good; where is the light and where is the honey? Although these might be the most difficult questions to seriously ask yourself in times of difficulty, they are questions that turn us back to the 'somehow' goodness of God. They are questions that give us hope.

I had to ask these questions at the end of that first university term as I found myself on Holy Trinity Church's student house party, a weekend away of worship, prayer and spending fun time together. On the second evening, the night before my birthday, my parents phoned me to tell me that my grandad had died.

He had been ill for a long time; it was expected. I knew him, but I didn't know him well – we were not super close. These things that people sometimes say to soften the blow of death all ran through my head... and had no softening effect. I ended up in tears (the second uncharacteristic church-crying time at Holy Trinity), and sat with Ellie, who listened and prayed for me, praying peace and comfort in the midst of grief. Death tears a hole that feels irreparable.

I dried my eyes and ran upstairs to put comfy pyjamas on. Still dazed, I headed to our evening of late night worship – an hour of open-mic singing and praying. The worship team led us in a couple of songs before playing music to invite worship; there was a microphone standing in the middle for anyone to take and speak from if they felt they had a prayer or a word from God to share with the room.

I usually shy away from such spontaneous microphone speaking and praying, having had some unhelpful past experiences. However, it was the first time I'd experienced open-mic at Holy Trinity and I felt safer here. It was the first time I felt myself undeniably and irresistibly drawn to the mic, too – literally, I found myself halfway across the room before I'd even had chance to think about it!

And, so, I found myself, tired-eyed from tears, emotionally shattered and wearing pyjamas, standing with a mic in my hand, proclaiming light's victory over darkness to a roomful of worshipping people. 'In this world, we are all going to face hard things,' I said, 'yet in Jesus there is hope that conquers even death. The songs that we sing in worship become our victory cry: our God saves and he will not be overcome. "Light shines in the darkness and the darkness has not overcome it"' (John 1:5).

Confronted with the reality of death, my comfort came from the truth that God's light always overcomes darkness. We so clearly see it in Christ, and we can clearly see it in him even in the midst of difficult struggle. His are the wounds that we can put our hands into and know that he feels our pain with us: 'He takes into heaven [his] wounded body, so that God might always and for ever know what it is like to feel the pain and suffering of our wounded humanity.'[33]

So, draw close to the God who is with you and get familiar with what his grace looks like, even in tough situations. Some friends and I used the analogy of our university studies to think about this: just as we all get familiar with the principles of the subjects we're studying through the time we spend learning and practising them, so we get familiar with who God is as we spend time with him. For the mathematician, Emily, familiarity grew when she practised the formulae over and over, learning to spot patterns and correlations. For the classicist learning ancient Greek, another Emily, familiarity with the language grew as she learned to recognise grammatical patterns. For the geologist, recognition of different rocks grew as he learned their various properties, their patterns of shape, feel, smell – and even taste. He grew familiar through spending time getting to know his subject inside out.

It was this geologist, Matt, who summarised the analogy for us all: 'It's like, through prayer and spending time with God, we grow familiar with the sound of God's voice, and we begin to hear him more and more.' *We grow familiar with the sound of God's voice*: and we hear him weep with us as we grieve; draw near to us in our worry; speak love over us when we feel too down-and-out to keep going. Press into his grace through prayer: with honey from the rock he will satisfy you.

At this chapter's close, I'll return to the house party. I was given brilliant confirmation of God's goodness after I'd stood at the mic and proclaimed light's victory (in my pyjamas). A friend, Lucy, came up to me and she gave me a scrap of paper with just one verse written on it: 'Who is this coming up from the wilderness leaning on her beloved?' (Song of Solomon 8:5).

Lean on the one who loves you as you wander through the wilderness. You will come out the other side knowing more deeply about him, your roots grown deeper down in his grace.

Headphones time

It can be difficult to pray through the hard things. Here are some questions and things you could do to begin to think about how God's with you in all things.

- 'Rejoice always, pray continually, give thanks in all circumstances; for this is God's will for you in Christ Jesus' (1 Thessalonians 5:16–18). Pray about the circumstances in which you find it more difficult to rejoice, pray and give thanks.

- Read Mary Oliver's poem 'Breakage'. What story has God written through difficult times you've encountered in the past?

- Find a smallish, pocket-sized stone and a permanent marker (nail varnish also works). Write 'honey' across the stone and take it with you as a reminder that God brings honey from the rock, sweetness from the hard places, wherever you go. Read and reflect on the story of 'stones to remind the people' in Joshua 41:1–9.

- Someone once said to me: 'Dig the wells in the good times, because then, in the tricky times where there's no water, you can drink from the wells you've dug already.' If you're in a good place right now, what could you do to 'dig the wells' so that, when the tricky times come, you have 'water' to sustain you?

- Are you still processing a time that was really tricky? Perhaps you could write it down as a story, as I did above; write it as a path of hope heading out of the wilderness place, following God's footsteps.

Soundtrack

'Whatever comes' by Rend Collective and 'In the night' by Andrew Peterson.

I don't need to say anything about these; just listen and hear God speak.

These words are your life

Finding God in the Bible

God wrote, 'I love you' – he wrote it in the sky, on the earth and under the sea... And God put it into words, too, and wrote it in a book called 'the Bible'.[34]

'They are not just idle words for you – they are your life. By them you will live long in the land you are crossing the Jordan to possess.' So, Moses concludes his song to the Israelites in Deuteronomy 32:47. He has reminded them of God's faithful actions and has encouraged them to embrace his promises of both judgement and renewal. He has described the law as gentle rain falling to refresh new grass, showers that bring new life, growth and goodness (v. 2). *These words are your life*, he says, these words from God are the words that will refresh, teach and guide you. They are the words that will govern your life as they light up the path for your feet, and they will help you to walk with integrity, truth and grace. They are the words that will lead you into the land that God has promised you – take them to heart and obey them carefully. They are your life.

In the New Testament, we see it again: 'All scripture is God-breathed and is useful for teaching, rebuking, correcting and training in righteousness, so that the servant of God may be thoroughly equipped for every good work' (2 Timothy 3:16–17). Paul writes these words to Timothy in reference to the Old Testament, the scripture the early church held in their hands – but now, as we hold our Bibles in *our* hands, comprising both Old and New Testaments, we know that *all* scripture is God-breathed, from Genesis to Revelation. *All* of these words are our life, shaping us to be more Christlike as we read them, absorb them and take them into our hearts.

Indeed, these words are 'more precious than gold, than much pure gold; they are sweeter than honey, than honey from the honeycomb' (Psalm 19:10). These words are the means by which God speaks to us, guiding us in righteousness by showing up our sin and his grace, by pointing us always to Jesus. As such, these words are our treasure, our more-precious-than-gold gift. They help us to know God's heart and they sustain us as we take them in; they are sweeter than honey, which, as we saw in the last chapter, is really rather sweet and good and sustaining.

These are three places I turn to in the Bible to remind myself of what the Bible is and how important it is to read, study and know it. Because of these verses and others like them, I believe that the Bible is God's voice speaking to us; reading it creates a space in which we can listen and talk to God himself. You might have some questions about these beliefs – perhaps you're wondering about where the Bible's authority comes from, who wrote each book in it or who decided which books would be included. If these are your questions, or if you have similar questions, jot them down – and then head to the Recommendations on page 150. I've included some resources that will help you to think through these issues, as in this chapter I'm going to take the approach of telling you stories about how the words of the Bible have changed my, or my friends', lives, rather than discussing why the Bible is like it is. (Although it's immensely fascinating, this is a question too big to discuss in one short chapter!)

As I tell these stories, I'll discuss points from them which could help you think about how you could read the Bible – I'll mention questions of genre, context and Bible translations while drawing out really practical ways you can get stuck into God's word. It's not an exhaustive list; rather, it's a starting point to help you ask questions about the Bible. As you read, think about your own experiences: how have you heard God's voice through his word?

A couple of years ago at Christmastime, my godmother recommended Tim Keller's book *My Rock, My Refuge: A year of daily devotions in the psalms*. With some friends from her church, she had decided to read it throughout the following year – she invited me and my family to join them. This is how I found myself committed to reading the psalms for a year, with help from Tim Keller's book.

By the end of the year, I'd read all the psalms and had found God there – I had seen new aspects of his character and had engaged with his grace in a way that was new to me. It was new, because I had never before committed to reading God's word in such a consistent way over such a long period of time. Yet I found that the commitment and structure really helped me – it meant that I opened the Bible on (nearly every) day of the year, even when I didn't particularly feel like it. And this was good; it kept me in the habit of seeking God.

This doesn't mean, however, that I read the Bible in the same way every day. Sometimes, in busier weeks, I just let the words wash over me and give me rest; at other times, I dug deeper into the passage and asked questions about what each word meant. The one thing that remained the same was that God met me when I opened his word with a heart open to hearing his voice. He spoke to me through the Bible as I sought him through it.

Another helpful element of this experience was that I wasn't doing it alone. Commitment is trickier when no one is walking alongside you. With my godmother committed to reading the same passages as me every day, I felt encouraged to keep going. With Keller's words providing a different perspective, I didn't get stuck inside my own thoughts. This is the value of doing things together: we can all encourage each other to keep seeking God in fresh ways. I totally recommend committing to reading a book of the Bible alongside your friends, and I also recommend finding a good devotional book to help you to see passages in new ways. (Devotionals, or Bible study notes, are great because they have little explanations or reflections on the passage for the day, and maybe some questions to help you reflect on it yourself. They are some of the best resources for helping you to understand parts of the Bible – check the Recommendations on page 150 for some that I've found useful.)

The fact that there was one passage for each day helped as well: because I like things to be finished, I was constantly motivated not to miss a day. My friend Rachel also noticed this in her Bible reading rhythm:

> I need holding to account – I am motivated by being able to complete things nicely. This is incredibly useful because knowing that if I do not set aside time to read the Bible then I will have to leave a blank on certain pages [of my journal] does give me a good *incentive to make sure the time is set aside*.[35]

A final point about my year in the psalms is about genre, the type of text. Psalms is a collection of poems which were written to be sung as responses to life experiences. Some are inspired by particular historical or personal events in the life of God's people; some are general reflections on life, us and God; all can be reused and reinterpreted as the personal prayers of anyone. Arthur, one of my university supervisors, once said that since the fall (Genesis 3) we don't feel right – yet psalms, he continued, help us to feel better by acting as vehicles for our own prayers. They help us to align our feelings with God's heart by giving us words to pray with, words for us to express our emotions – sorrow, anger, shame, praise, thanksgiving – while allowing us to be held in God's grace and comfort. The tensions of life and the whole range of human emotions are found in the psalms: they remind us that 'it is okay to express to God all these conflicting emotions, even at the same time. They say something profound about the deep paradoxes of life, including my highly contradictory feelings about my relationship with God,'[36] as one retired pastor writes.

My year in the psalms thus showed me how to take my feelings to God and let him weave his grace into them. The genre of the text itself helped me to grow roots in God's grace.

Biblical genres other than psalm-poetry include: history, wisdom, law, prophecy, narrative, parable, revelation and epistles (letters). The genre of the Bible book you choose to read must direct how you read it – you can't read a letter like a psalm; Leviticus cannot be read in the same way as John. Gordon D. Fee and Douglas Stuart have written a fantastic book called *How to Read the Bible for All Its Worth* (Zondervan, 2003) which explains different biblical genres and how to approach them; here, to illustrate different approaches to genre, I'll tell another story. This time it's about reading a letter: how does my reading of it differ to how I read the psalms?

——————— ▪ ■ ▪ ———————

1 Peter is a short epistle found near the end of the New Testament. It's written by Peter to a handful of churches scattered 'throughout the provinces of Pontus, Galatia, Cappadocia, Asia and Bithynia' (1:1), and it's full of challenge and encouragement from Peter for his readers to live up to their identity in Christ.

I studied this letter with my college Christian Union in my first term as college representative (one of the two college Christian Union leaders). As I planned each Bible study with my co-rep, I got to know the letter really well – and then I got to see it in a whole new light as we discussed it with the group. Each person bought their own perspective and thoughts, and we were always surprised by the truth and grace uncovered through dialogue.

For example, we got a sense of the difficulties faced by Peter's readers as we explored particular parts of the text. 4:12–19 dwells on suffering for being Christian, and 5:8 specifies the threat of the devil who 'prowls around like a roaring lion looking for someone to devour'. While discussing this phrase, someone explained that lions hunt those who wander alone, away from the pack; this realisation challenged us to grow closer as a God-centred, joy-full and fearless community who support and encourage each other in faith.

Digging into the Bible together, by asking questions of both its original context and current relevance, really helped us to grow roots in God's grace, both individually and as a community. Discussion and wrestling enabled us to see God in so many new, practical, strong ways, moving us to apply his truth to our lives.

Such wrestling with passages can take many forms – meditating on one verse at a time; discussion with others; academic study; reading books and commentaries on particular passages. This pursuit of truth bears fruit even in the unlikeliest of places; you find treasure more precious than gold even in the seemingly more obscure books of the Bible.

Stu, a student worker at church, once excitedly chatted with a group of us about how much he was learning from Leviticus – and I just looked wide-eyed and incredulous because… Leviticus? Really? The most I'd heard about Leviticus was that it is the book most people get stuck at when they try to read the Bible in a year. Yet here was Stu, telling us he spent a chunk of his day in Leviticus, wrestling with the book's complicated imagery and finding God within it.

The challenge here is to choose the more difficult books of the Bible and get equipped to read them – because God is in Leviticus as much as he is in Philippians. Stu mentioned two commentaries which really helped him to study Leviticus;[37] why don't you, the next time you're finding the Bible hard to understand, gather some wise and keen friends and find a good commentary that unpacks the tricky parts with you? The Bible is accessible to all of us: pursue truth in it. Listen for God's voice, whether that involves just sitting and being with the words or grappling and wrestling with them instead.

Whatever you do, be really intentional about what you read. I've found again and again that I read the Bible more if I've decided beforehand what I'll look at; if I open the Bible but don't know where to start, I often end up closing the covers again and ignoring God's word for the day. To avoid this, I tend to create and commit to following a 'reading plan' that lasts about 60 days – you can often find pre-created ones in the front or back of your Bible, or on the internet.

If planning something like this is helpful for you, go for it. If not, experiment with different ideas until you find something that suits you. Or if you think it could be helpful, but are not sure what Bible book to start your plan with, why not begin with the gospels? Matthew, Mark, Luke and John are full of stories of what Jesus said and did, who he was, how his life, death and resurrection was foretold throughout the Old Testament. John's gospel even begins with a play on the Genesis creation account: 'In the beginning was the Word,' John writes before launching into one of the most earth-shattering pieces of prose ever written. This continual connection between Old and New Testament helps you to begin to understand how the Bible fits together – Jesus is the centre and from stories of him springs exploration of the rest of God's word.

I'd also like to say that the gospels, and indeed any Bible book, can never be too 'overfamiliar' or 'over-read'. Margaret White, who has been a Christian for her whole life, writes:

> Last year, I only read the gospels, which was so interesting and challenging, as well as a real blessing. I spent one whole weekend on John 15, which talks about Jesus being the vine. It taught me again that our purpose is to bear fruit – and I think as Christians we all want to do this, wherever we are.[38]

Margaret saw 'again', freshly, what God was calling her to do, even though she'd probably read John 15 plenty of times before. My friend Nathan tells a similar story:

A few months ago, God spoke powerfully to me through a sermon on a familiar verse, Matthew 5:6. I suppose I'd always previously passed over this quickly as just one of the nice-sounding statements of the beatitudes, but God suddenly opened my eyes to my need to genuinely hunger after his righteousness. In reality, I've always been in need of more of God's righteousness in my life… but how often have I felt that as a pressing hunger and thirst, a need that I can't afford to leave unsatisfied?

A verse oft-skimmed over, heard again, became a 'regular reminder' about pursuing righteousness and recognising his need for it. If you don't know where to begin, read familiar passages again – what will you see differently?

Nathan's story also captures that feeling of sudden realisation, that jolt when words seem to jump off the page or out from the sermon and speak straight into your heart. I don't know if you've ever felt that before, the sense that the words of the Bible perfectly fit or deeply challenge what you're thinking about, praying through or experiencing. It's like when the two men on the road to Emmaus suddenly recognised Jesus, when he took and broke the bread. They asked: 'Were not our hearts burning within us while he talked with us on the road and opened the scriptures to us?' (Luke 24:32).

Our hearts burn within us sometimes as we open up the Bible. God awakens us to deep truth, opening our eyes and causing us to recognise or realise something of him. It's hard to explain, but it's beautiful and good – as you read the Bible, ask God to show you what he's saying to you and to give you the certainty that the men travelling to Emmaus felt, and that Nathan felt as he listened to the sermon on Matthew 5:6.[39] Ask him to help you to choose where and how to hear him in his word.

A final story for this chapter comes from my friend Eri, a fellow leader at summer camp. We were planning a talk for 8–11-year-olds, so we looked to see if the Bible story we were speaking on was in *The Jesus Storybook Bible*, a great Bible retelling for children, by Sally Lloyd-Jones. It wasn't, but we spent a few minutes just chatting about the *Storybook Bible*. Eri loves it, and reads it with her young mums group. The simple words and beautiful pictures are perfect for reading with their small (and adorable) children; all of the mums love it and see God through it. There's this one beautiful phrase that Eri read to me about God's love, a phrase that is repeated throughout the whole text. After the Lord's Prayer, it appears like this: 'You see, Jesus was showing people that God would always love them – with a Never Stopping, Never Giving Up, Unbreaking, Always and Forever Love.'[40]

This conversation showed me that we can know God in the Bible through different translations of the same text, slight variations pointing to the same truth at different levels. *The Jesus Storybook Bible* illuminates God's love through beautiful illustrations and easy language; the NIV balances closeness to the original languages with modern colloquialisms and interpretation. *The Message* is another alternate rendering, leaning much more on interpretive than linguistic translation – yet it draws so many people into the space of hearing God speak truth into their lives. When you come to reading the Bible, think about what translation you're using. Is it an accurate translation that relies on biblical and linguistic research? Does it help you to understand the text? Does it make it easier or harder for you to know God through his word? Is there a translation that your church recommends or uses?

We can know God through the Bible in so many different ways. We can know him through our individual daily devotional times; through wrestling with the text either alone or in a group; through hearing God's word spoken in a sermon; through having our eyes opened by his grace to the 'wonderful things in his law' (Psalm 119:18). These 'wonderful things' are vast and many – the Bible is the book of a lifetime, always showing us something new of the depths of who God is. My mate Phil writes:

The Bible, a mentor once told me, 'is a pool both shallow enough for toddlers to play yet deep enough for elephants to bathe'. This I found to be true since it was first read to me at bedtime when I was a toddler. Through its words, I learned about the God who made the universe... As I grew older, perplexing questions I had about morality and human purpose were made clearer, as the Bible explained our rebellion from God and the hope of reconciliation Jesus offers. Most wonderful of all, though, is Jesus. Through the Bible's pages, we meet the Creator of the universe, and when we hear him speak, every thought in our mind is stilled to the wonders he utters.

Jesus speaks through his word, showing us wonders, and he longs to speak to *you* and transform you into the person he's made you to be. Crack open the cover of a Bible, choose a book, say a prayer, grab some friends or a commentary, if you'd like, and get reading. He's waiting for you there.

Headphones time

Here are some further questions to help you pray and think through the value of the Bible and fresh ways you could seek God in it.

- How would you explain what the Bible is to someone who has never heard of it before? What stories could you tell them of how God speaks through it?

- What new ideas have the stories in this chapter given you about how to read the Bible? Choose a couple and commit to trying them out in the next week or two.

- Psalm 119 is the longest psalm, and it's all about the beauty, value and goodness of the word of God. Read a little of it each day over the next few weeks and reflect on its themes.

- Have a think about what time in the day could be best for reading God's word. Are you most awake in the morning or the evening? Do you have a long train or bus journey every day that you could put aside for Bible time?

- Read and spend some time dwelling on Luke 24:13–34. Wouldn't it be amazing to hear Jesus' own Bible overview, all pointing to himself (v. 27)? One good question to ask about whatever passage you're reading is this: 'How does this point to Jesus?' Try it the next time you read the Bible.

Soundtrack

'Your ways' by Holy Trinity Worship

This song helps me to release my own agendas into God's hands, and let his wisdom direct how I read his word.

Story stop: Worry people

This is the second story stop, another time to pause and reflect on something from when I was younger. This time, the memory is from when I was about nine or ten and still at primary school, and it's about how worry can be turned into prayer. What do you worry about, and how have you learned to pray about worry?

Head on pillow, eyes closed, duvet pulled up to chin. Comfortable in pyjamas at the end of the day, the light fading to black outside until the bright glory of morning will surprise everyone's blinking eyes. Restful sleep from now until then is exactly what I need.

I shuffle down and get comfortable – and that's when the thoughts start buzzing: 'Oh yeah, that thing that happened at school today! Jack made fun of me again and what if it carries on tomorrow? But it's okay, I know I have friends too. I hope they stay my friends, even when we start thinking about new, big schools.

Friends – that game at lunch was so fun, it was great pretending to be lions on the hunt for elephants! It's like the programme I saw for my animals project – hmmm, I wonder how I'll get that done? I want it to be perfect…'

And on (and on) it goes. My eyes open wide because I'm thinking so much; my brain won't switch off and sleep won't come. Rest's a dream, and dreams are far away.

Just as I'm starting to despair, there appears a golden, solid slice of light shining in from the landing. Mum looks in around the door: 'Not asleep yet?'

'No,' I say, and sit up. 'My brain won't switch off tonight, again.'

'Have you tried thinking about something else?'

'Yes! I try that. Every. Single. Night. It doesn't work, ever!'

'Hannah, I'm not quite sure what to suggest – unless... wait a minute.'

Mum closes the door, leaving quiet darkness to enfold my busy brain again. Just as I think she's taking too long, the solid light slices across the floor once more. Mum comes and sits on the edge of my bed, and in her hand is a little yellow box. She opens the lid and tips some tiny dolls out on to her hand. They're smaller than the tip of my littlest finger.

'Hannah, these are called worry people. Before you go to bed, you can whisper one of the things that keeps you awake to each of the worry people. They'll take it away and look after it overnight so you don't have to think about it when you're trying to get to sleep.'

I take the box from my mum's hand as she smiles and leaves the room. Sitting tousle-haired in the dark, I line up the worry people on my duvet. Their bright colours stand out in the dark; one by one I take a worry person and whisper in its ear.

'Jack's been worrying me – he makes fun of me at school and I don't know what to do.'

'I have a big animal project to finish and I don't know where to start.'

'My friends – I hope we keep having fun even when we go to secondary school.'

I put each worry person in the box after whispering to them. When I finish, I put the box under my pillow. I close my eyes, shuffle down and slowly drift into dreams.

———————— ▫▪▫ ————————

The worry people became for me a way of praying, a rhythm of whispering my worries to God. For a child with a big imagination, the worry people were really helpful – a good way to visualise speaking to God.

Now, as an older person (still with a big imagination), I don't need the worry people – but I do have a 'sleep book'. I jot down all the things that keep me awake and then I put the book away. I know God hears our prayers and worries, however we tell them to him. We don't have to stay awake because God stays awake for us – he who watches over us never slumbers nor sleeps (Psalm 121).

6

Approaching the throne

The practice and power of prayer

Real prayer comes not from gritting our teeth but from falling in love.[41]

God's throne stands there, golden and grand, tall and beautiful and holy.

An impenetrable sheet of glass stands between the throne and the person; the person can look, but they cannot enter and touch. God's throne stands there unapproachable, irreproachable.

As the person looks on, the sheet of glass suddenly shatters in a cascade of glittering sound and light.

And they know, immediately. They know that God's throne stands there – and they can touch it. They are invited into the throne room of God; nothing stands in their way.

This picture was shared with me by a girl in my dorm on summer camp a few years ago. I don't know where she is now or what God has been doing in her life – but in that moment, she saw, in a startling vision, that God loved her and invited her to draw near to him.

Prayer is beautifully this: approaching 'God's throne of grace with confidence, so that we may receive mercy and find grace to help us in our time of need' (Hebrews 4:16). As Richard Foster writes, prayer is the key that allows us to enter the home that is God's heart; prayer allows us to enter the door that is Jesus Christ, so that we may boldly approach God's golden and grand, tall and beautiful and holy throne.[42]

At his throne, we find rest. We find comfort in times of trouble; challenge to live holy lives; strength to obey God's word; dreams and visions of creativity that inspire us to seek and embody God's kingdom. In prayer, we receive from God's hand the joy and wisdom that he longs to give us. In prayer, we draw near to the Father-heart of God and find that he delights in us and sings over us with love.

This doesn't mean that prayer is easy. Perhaps prayerlessness is more familiar to you than prayerfulness. You can't find the words; you don't know where to begin; you feel too inadequate to pray; you feel like you never get the words *just right*.

But remember the picture above: the person only looked. They didn't hit out at the glass and try to break it themselves; they didn't say the right combination of words to unlock the door into God's throne room. They only looked and accepted the invitation when it came.

I wrote in *God's Daughters* these words:

> God, not you, began this conversation. As Jesus breathed his last on the cross, the way opened up for you to converse with the divine. Luke 23:45 says that, as Jesus died, 'the curtain of the temple was torn in two'. The curtain had, for centuries, separated God's people from God's presence – and now the curtain was being torn apart. God was made accessible by Jesus' curtain-rending death.[43]

God was made accessible by Jesus' glass-shattering sacrifice. The way is open: whatever mixed-up, complicated place you're coming from and whatever messy, crazy words you use, God longs to hear you speak to him. He's big enough to listen to and understand your imperfect and incomplete prayers – and he has invited you into his throne room even before you opened your mouth to speak. He delights to hear whatever prayers you offer up to him – both the joyful and the sorrowful, the grateful and the angry. He is with you and he has made a way: will you walk in it?

My totally amazing friend Claire once said to me, with great surprise, that she had found that as she made space to pray and listen to God, God met and spoke to her. We looked at this in the chapter about habits and rhythms: carving out regular and intentional space to pray is so important in accepting God's invitation of grace. As you work out your salvation, through times of intentional prayer and Bible reading, God works in you. It's mutual, relational and not at all a one-sided thing. God works in you as you look to him; you look to God because he first invites you.

Here, we are going to look at a few ways in which you could use that intentional prayer space. We won't be looking at either praying in creation or the value of silence in prayer times because these topics both have their own chapters. Instead, we'll look at lots of other ways you can pray, remembering that prayer is not about earning God's attention or battling your way into his presence; rather, it's about accepting his invitation of grace and sitting down to chat with your Father.

Praying with scripture is something that I find really helpful, particularly with psalms or with specific phrases from my Bible reading for the day. One summer, Psalm 23 became a rock for me as it guided and directed my prayers through different travels and adventures. I prayed it with friends in the Round Church in Cambridge, taking one verse at a time to show us what to give thanks for. We were reassured of the certain victory we have in Christ by praying with God's own words.

I prayed it in the Assisi monastery, sitting overlooking the valley and turning over the words in my heart. God surely does make us lie down in green pastures: praying through his word prompted me to give thanks and choose joy.

I prayed it at summer camp as another leader read it out from *The Message* in an evening meeting. God is true to his word, and his word realigns my prayers to his truth. I prayed it as a friend blogged[44] about each verse for 15 days, and I learned again that God is with me. I prayed it as I enjoyed a book written by a shepherd[45] as a reflection on the psalm, sitting in a holiday cottage in Cornwall.

You can pray with scripture like this too, noticing repetitions and patterns as you go about your daily life. Maybe choose a psalm or a verse to recall every time you find yourself in a new place. Memorise it; bring it to mind when you're feeling a bit lost at sea and need something solid to hold on to. This is often how God teaches us to pray: by giving us secure, solid words to remind us of truth and help our hearts to trust him.

Another way that scripture has helped me to pray is when I've prayed for others by using Bible verses. I ask God what he'd like me to pray for someone, and wait and listen to see what he says. Sometimes nothing happens, and I just pray with my own words; sometimes God helps me to see how a specific verse would be good to pray for someone in the situation that they're in. Occasionally, I share that verse as an encouragement with that person; often, I keep it to myself and just pray it over them each day.

For example, this morning I was praying for friends who are on exciting summer adventures by using these words from Jude 20–21 (MSG):

> But you, dear friends, carefully build yourselves up in this most holy faith by praying in the Holy Spirit, staying right at the centre of God's love, keeping your arms open and outstretched, ready for the mercy of our Master, Jesus Christ. This is the unending life, the *real* life.

These words shaped my prayers, leading me to specifically ask God to strengthen my friends in their prayer and open-armed surrender to Jesus. Praying like this also shows me how best to support and encourage others, reminding me to keep in touch with them as they adventure to new places. Praying for others builds up God's church. Why don't you choose three friends to pray for and ask God what he'd like you to pray for them?

As you pray, whether it's by using scripture or your own words, remember that prayer can be as creative and different as you would like it to be. Prayer isn't just about sitting with your eyes closed and hands together, quietly saying words to God – although it can be all these things. Prayer is about an attitude of coming continually and humbly into God's awesome presence; it's not about strictly or legalistically following a specific method or practice. You can try lots of different and creative ways of spending time with God – however you accept his invitation, he's always waiting there to listen and speak with you.

Summer camp is one place where I've experienced the most variety of creative ways to pray. In our leaders' meeting before the kids arrive, we worship and pray together. One year we prayed by doing messy clay modelling; another year we prayed with buttons. Each of us chose a button and gave thanks for as many things as there were holes in the button. We grouped together with people who had the same colour or shape button, and we prayed in these groups for the week ahead. It was useful to have something to fiddle with and focus on as we brought our requests to God.

At other times, we have encouraged the children to pray creatively. We've had big sheets of paper and lots of pens so that they can draw or write their prayers. We've had a prayer station where you can post worries into a cardboard postbox to symbolically give them to God. We've seen kids dancing outside to classic worship tunes like Rend Collective's 'My Lighthouse', praising God by doing actions and singing loud.

In college Christian Union, we've sometimes adopted creative prayer as well, using Lego blocks to think about how each of us are living stones built up into God's church (1 Peter 2). We've used mirrors to quite literally reflect on our identity in Jesus: first, we wrote on the mirrors the words that we and our friends would use to describe ourselves; second, we rubbed them off and replaced them with the words God uses to describe us.

Such simple activities can often help you to focus on what you're praying for or about. God uses and loves our creativity and he gives us freedom to speak to him in any language – whether that's the language of Lego and playing or the language of speaking out our words and prayers to him.

If you think this creative approach could be good for you, go for it! Get some paint and paper and spend some time painting your prayers. Put some music on and sing to God; do actions if that helps you to listen and respond to him. Grab a notebook and some pens and 'prayer journal'. I have a friend, Becky, who spends time listening to God by drawing in a notebook. She draws a picture of the core theme of what she's praying about on one page of the notebook. She then writes a description of the picture on the opposite page to help her pray it through.

God gives us this freedom and ability to create, reflect and listen to him in the way that suits us the best. For some, that will be writing or playing music; for others, silent reflection with closed eyes might be the most helpful way to pray. The way you pray might be different at different times – for me, in the busyness of university term times, painting my responses and prayers comes more easily to me than praying with words. This is because most of my day at university consists of reading and writing, and to paint my responses is a way of doing something different to rest with God and think more slowly.

This all leads to the question: how do I know if a particular way to pray is helpful for me, in this time and this place? How do I know if I'm praying my best prayers?

You can answer this question as we have before, by thinking about how prayer fits into the rhythm of your life and building up habits that are sensitive to your whole life. You can also answer this question like this: you know you're praying your best prayers when you're transformed by God through them. You know that your roots are growing deep in God's grace when your character and life begins to bear the 'multifaceted fruit'[46] of the Spirit, when you begin to be formed in the likeness of Christ. Foster writes:

> To pray is to change. This is a great grace. How good of God to provide a path whereby our lives can be taken over by love and joy and peace and patience and kindness and goodness and faithfulness and gentleness and self-control.[47]

Through the intimacy with God that prayer engenders, we are transformed. Prayer takes our weaknesses and breathes strength into them as we experience God's powerful grace. Prayer shifts our perspective from the hopelessness of life without God to the immense hopefulness of life with him. Prayer writes truth on to our very souls and teaches our hearts to beat to God's rhythm – it's the most powerful action we can take in any and every situation as it both calls upon the sovereign Creator of the universe to act, *and* changes us so that we are the vessels of that same Creator.

Prayer is how we become who we are: God's children; his hands and feet; his light to those in darkness; his ambassadors to those who don't yet dwell in his kingdom. Without prayer, we forget our identity and lose our strength. With prayer, we claim God's victory in every area of our lives as we align ourselves humbly with him.

This is truly incredible. So, let's pray believing it.

Often, we don't pray as if we mean it or as if we believe that prayer is really that powerful. Because we may not see immediate or expected results or get a certain feeling about what we've just prayed, we can often lose motivation with prayer, forgetting that

God hears every single word that we pray, and catches every single tear that we cry, and even understands our wordless prayers that we groan when we run out of the means and energy to express ourselves. We forget that God is big and powerful and good, that he loves us and is with us and longs to see his kingdom come in our lives and communities.

So, let's learn to pray believing that God really does transform us and our world in some beautiful way through the prayers that we bring.

I am reminded of the Tuesday evening following the awful attack in Manchester on 22 May 2017 which killed 22 people. The student contingent of our church congregation had gathered like always to worship, pray and read God's word together. This evening was different; the worship time was extended as one of the student workers prayed for the unfolding situation in Manchester, for the victims and their families, the emergency services and the surrounding community.

After each short prayer, we were invited to sing our response to the words and tune of the opening chorus of Bethel's 'We Will Not Be Shaken'.[48] With each prayer and response, the sound in the room grew and grew and we all knew deep down that our prayers, prayed 180 miles away from the emergency, had more power in the situation in Manchester than the likes, retweets or comforting messages that had been flooding in.

Our prayers had the power to push back the darkness and bring hope in a terrible situation. They were not words sent into the void, but trusting, hopeful requests sung out to an incredible God. Somehow God hears our prayers, honours them and works through them to bring about amazing things that are more powerful than we could ask or imagine.

It's like the time during Escape and Pray, when I sat with Holly, Miriam and Flora in a quiet metro station on the outskirts of Madrid, late at night and with an hour of travelling ahead of us. Holly, usually chatty and bubbly, was growing quieter as we waited for the train – she explained that her heatstroke from the night before had returned, and it had returned bad.

Flora wrapped her hands around Holly's hurting head and prayed for Jesus to give her the healing that she needed. Holly took painkillers, knowing that they wouldn't kick in for another 20 minutes.

Ten seconds after Flora prayed, Holly sat up with tears in her eyes. Her headache had completely disappeared and her eyesight was normal again, and she was back to her bubbly self. The four of us sat in that metro station, stunned by such an incredible answer to prayer in a time of real need.

Prayer is powerful because the God who hears and sees is mighty and loving. Our best prayers grow us into the people God wants us to be: people who trust him for all things and who are obedient to his voice.

I realise that this short exploration of such a deep topic skims over some of the tricky, more complicated questions about prayer. What about different types of prayer – intercession, lament, petition or thanksgiving? For that, try Foster's *Prayer* (Hodder & Stoughton, 2008) or Keller's *Prayer* (Hodder & Stoughton, 2014). What happens when it feels like God is not answering our prayers? Instead of trying to answer that now, I'll direct you to Pete Greig's book *God on Mute* (Kingsway Publications, 2007), and leave you with this quote from C.S. Lewis who, when his wife was dying, was asked why he prays if God does not answer.

> That's not why I pray. I pray because I can't help myself. I pray because I'm helpless. I pray because the need flows out of me all the time, waking and sleeping. It doesn't change God. It changes me.[49]

Prayer changes us. God's love transforms us; his golden and grand, tall and beautiful and holy throne stands there, and we are invited to go and be with him.

Headphones time

The best way to learn how to pray is just to start praying – which is why I'll leave you now with some 'headphones time' and a soundtrack or two, to help you think through what you've just read.

- Read through the Lord's Prayer, the prayer Jesus taught his disciples (Luke 11:1–4 or Matthew 6:9–13). What captures your attention about how Jesus teaches the disciples to address God?

- What type of learner are you? Do you engage more with visual, auditory or kinaesthetic (active and practical) styles of teaching? How could you use this knowledge about how you learn to shape your prayer life?

- Check out the different suggestions and stories about how to pray on the 24–7 prayer website (www.24-7prayer.com/helpmepray). Choose two from either that website or this chapter that you will try out in the next few days.

- Think about your experiences of prayer. Have there been times when God has answered you in amazing ways, or does prayer feel more like an experience of watching, waiting and hoping to hear? How do your experiences encourage and challenge you to keep praying?

- Read through Psalms 145, 138, 86 and 51. What are the themes and mood of each psalm? How could the different types of prayer represented here help you to bring different feelings and requests to God?

Soundtrack

'Come ye sinners' by Sojourn Music and 'Come as you are' by Crowder.

I love these songs. Together, they capture the essence of God's invitation to us so clearly: lay down your burdens and your worries; come to him just as you are.

7

At home in the world

Knowing the Creator through his creation

Creation becomes a kind of gift, an offering prepared by God for awakening and illuminating our bodies and minds and spirits.[50]

Sand saturated with saltwater ran silkily over her feet and in between her toes, burying them a few millimetres deeper with each wave. The water was cold, but her skin had become indifferent; she had been crouching in this sandy hollow between a handful of boulders for the best part of an hour. Seaweed slicked over the surface of the rocks, its slippery ubiquity only occasionally interrupted by encrustations of barnacles, small and dimpled and hard. On the rock, directly in front of her, the barnacles and seaweed gave way to a blue-grey dappled expanse of glistening stone. She gazed intently at it while the sea lapped around, becoming perceptibly lower with every few waves. The tide was going out.

From a distance, it would seem as if the girl was looking only at a rock. But if you make your way across the sand towards her, barefoot, you'll begin to see that this isn't quite true. You'll glimpse a bright orange smudge, gleaming on the rock for a second before disappearing again, as if it were a trick of the light or a mistake of your sight. As you get closer, you'll see that it isn't a mistake or a trick – the orange smudge is real, disappearing only as the waves rise up above it, a rare occasion. Crouching down in the shallow water next to the girl, you'll realise finally that the smudge is in fact a starfish, its five fat tentacles clinging and glistening and covered in tiny white spots.

Watch awhile; this is not a waste of your time, to watch a starfish. Watch as it slowly moves towards the sea; explore with your eyes its pale orange-white underside as it raises a tentacle for a moment before clamping it back down on the rock. Smile as you taste salt air on your tongue and see the starfish lower a tentative tentacle into the water before raising it back up again, as if it were a reluctant swimmer entering for the first time into the pool.

Leave the starfish there for a while as it moves slowly down the rock into the waves. We'll return to it later, salt air around us again and imagination our guide. By then, we'll have explored how nature or creation can help us to pray and spend time with God.

Being in nature might not be the most obvious way to pray that you can think of. It may even seem completely counterintuitive. The poet Gerard Manley Hopkins is an extreme example; although he is now known for fantastic poems which have creation as their subject, he burned a lot of his early work because he thought that he focused too much on nature and not enough on God. Nature, he felt, should 'buckle under' religion[51] – it was only later on that he came to read nature alongside the revelation of the Bible.

Nature and God should not be pitted against each other like this: God created nature and we can experience him through it. Creation is often the place in which people feel most 'at home', most free to be themselves. It is a place of connectedness – a space in which we experience connection both to ourselves and, most amazingly, to God, the Creator. As such, the Bible is rich in images taken from the natural world, using them in its teaching, praise and prayer. We see this from Genesis through to Revelation. In this chapter, we'll focus on just a couple of passages after exploring what it means to pray and experience God in nature.

When was the last time you went for a walk? Did you ramble long over fields and through woods, or did you just nip across town to the shops for some forgotten necessity? Do you remember the feel of fresh air on your skin – was it heavy with rain waiting to fall, or brilliant with blazing hot summer sunshine? Do you remember the feel of track or road under your feet, the constant thudding rhythm of your steps carrying you to dwell in the created world, however short your journey?

It's such a simple thing, the act of taking a walk – wherever and whenever this may be. You see things you'd never have noticed from your house or your car: the first spring buds; the smell of the pavement after rain; branches heavy with sweet autumn fruit; the sound of a roadside river bubbling through the town; the sight of the sky, always large and present whether you're a city dweller or a countryside rambler or something inbetween.

Not long ago, I holidayed with my family to an oft-returned-to spot on the north Norfolk coast. We stayed in my grandparents' caravan in a caravan park right on top of a hill. The hill overlooks the salty marshes: pools and rivers and long golden-green grasses; abandoned hulks of boats and driftwood; birds, lots of calling birds, with the occasional big brown cow. The marshes stretch and slump like this for miles, flat and relaxing on the eye, eventually giving way to the open sea, often grey and populated by seals.

A few steps outside the caravan park, there's a bench which overlooks all this wistful beauty and wildness; a plank of worn wood, weathered and smoothed by years of wind and rain and sun. It sits, unassuming, right on the edge of a crest in the hill. From a particular angle, it becomes the border between marsh and sky – the pale-gold-light-blue, incredible Norfolk sky.

It's on this bench that I found myself one sunset, lying on my back gazing up into the air. I'd been tied up in knots about something and needed the space to think and breathe, and so I lay there and, like Anne of Green Gables,[52] looked up into the big blue sky and just *felt* a prayer.

Wordlessly, I prayed and rested in the presence of God: God, made present through the colours of the sky; the feel of the evening breeze through my hair; the coconut-like smell from the nearby yellow thorny flowers. That's not to say that I have a pantheistic view of God – pantheism being a belief that God is literally creation, and creation is literally God. Rather, I'd say that God, although separate from creation, communicates through what he's created. His invisible kindness and beauty and love are made visible through the created world – and as I lay back on that worn old bench, that's what my heart came to know, wordlessly.

Read these words from Psalm 19:1–4:

> The heavens declare the glory of God;
>   the skies proclaim the work of his hands.
> Day after day they pour forth speech;
>   night after night they reveal knowledge.
> They have no speech, they use no words;
>   no sound is heard from them.
> Yet their voice goes out into all the earth,
>   their words to the ends of the world.

The sky – and all of creation – makes visible the invisible God. It becomes a gift and a communication of who God is and what his grace is like, revealing amazing knowledge about him. Paul writes to the Romans what the psalmist expresses in Psalm 19: 'Since the creation of the world God's invisible qualities – his eternal power and divine nature – have been clearly seen, being understood from what has been made, so that people are without excuse' (Romans 1:20). My time gazing up at the sunset sky was therefore a moment of prayer, of entering into relationship with God and listening to what he had to say to me about himself – and that time on the bench in the sunset untangled the knot inside me by showing me that, no matter what, God still keeps the earth spinning and the sun setting and rising; his faithfulness is forever and he watches over the safety of his people.

Another encounter with a sunset sky taught me the same truth: that God invites us to know him through what he's made. This time, the sky was on fire with reds and golds and pinks, fading slowly into deep star-studded blue at the other edge of the horizon. I was laughing much and walking carefree up a hill – with about 40 children and a bunch of more responsible people my own age and older. We were on camp and it was the first night; to wear everyone out before bed, we were going on a 'sunset hike', a super fun walk out the back of camp up to a field at the top.

We reached the field as I was chatting and catching up with another leader, Clare. We stopped with the rest of the group and gazed out into the sunset – and Clare laughingly introduced me to the wonderfully fun phrase 'awe time'. Awe time: a phrase coined by astronauts to describe time entirely dedicated to enjoying the incredible and beautiful views of earth from space.

I don't know if you followed Tim Peake's adventures in space in 2016. If you did, you'll have seen his stunning photos of earth from the space station: swirling clouds; sparkling city lights at night; the eerie green and pink aurora glow shadowing the planet's surface. Check out his Flickr or Facebook pages – and you'll see why 'awe time' is a near necessity. There's beauty in this place that's too good to miss.

We don't have to go up to space to experience 'awe time', this time of enjoying the wonder of it all and responding, often wordlessly, in awe and thanks and praise to the God who made it all. We can enjoy a fiery sunset with friends while on camp; lie back on benches and soak up the sky's beauty; pause to notice and dwell in the everyday beauty of the world while on walks to somewhere else. It's grace that surrounds us even when we're not aware of God's presence, grace that plays the sweetest song even when our ears are not tuned to hear it. Steven Chase writes: 'Out of some goodness and beauty and truth beyond imagining, God breathes into the nostrils of each living dragonfly, governing, cherishing, embodying and making of each a prayer.'[53] The grace of prayer and God's presence exists deeply in each dragonfly and creature he's created – and this is an incredible thing.

It's incredible because it means once more that rootedness in God's grace is available to everyone, and that it begins with God's invitation, initiative and amazing love rather than our own effort or strength. As we saw right at the start of this book, God has already given his all to us; this is evident in the beauty and provision of the natural world that each one of us can experience every day, whether that's by going outside or by watching nature documentaries (like *Planet Earth II* – would 100% recommend), or by experiencing art that's inspired by creation.

Growing roots in God's grace can therefore be about learning to listen to and see God's truth through the created world – and this is something every single person can do, whether they'd call themselves Christian or not. It's a grace undeserved by all: 'There is no way in which a man can earn a star or deserve a sunset';[54] stars and sunsets are gifts given directly from the hand of God. The whole of creation is a gift held out to you as you sit there reading these words; the invitation to see the invisible God through visible creation is yours. How will you choose to accept it?

We've mentioned a few ideas so far in this chapter: walking, sitting outside on benches, watching nature programmes, experiencing art. Here we'll explore a couple of these in more depth, and then look at the Bible to see how its writers have always used creation to communicate the grace of God.

Robert Macfarlane, author of beautiful books about nature, writes this: 'A walk is only a step away from a story, and every path *tells*.'[55]

Every path tells a story. They tell stories as our thoughts ramble with our footsteps, unravelling into something clearer than before. Not only do we notice the wonder of creation as we walk; the very act of walking in itself allows us to let go, empty our hands and be present before our Creator.

For me, at the moment, the rhythm of my feet reminds me of a heart beating: a heart beating love and life; God's heart healing mine, bringing forgiving peace to the hurting places and love and joy to all of me. These thoughts rise, effortlessly, as I walk to wherever I'm going, aware of God's presence in the world. Try it yourself: go for a walk and listen for God's voice in the rhythm of your steps, in the brush of wind through leaves, in the bright colours that make you smile. What do you discover as you walk? What story does the path tell?

As you walk and dwell in creation, you could try another way of accepting the gift of creation: creatively responding to the grace of God that you see. Compose poetry or stories as you wander, putting words together that somehow capture the glory of the world and express the feelings you have about it. Pick up leaves and trace their veins with your fingertips – with what intricacy and care God creates his world! Collect the leaves and stick them on your wall, to remind you of all you experience in nature. Perhaps take photos that hold within them the golden light of the sunrise or the bright purple of a tiny woodland flower. Look through the lens of a camera to see afresh the beauty of grace around you.

I have a friend who responds to God's grace shown in creation by wandering out to a field near her college to watch the sun set and sing songs of praise to God. The first time she did this, it was something that was completely new for her – it wasn't normal or expected, but in the end it was great, a wonderful time of praying by standing and singing in a wide-open field at sunset.

Another friend helps at a Christian outdoor activities site over the summer, encouraging and supporting families and mission teams as they grow together. With more focused teaching in the evening, the outside world is the main place they spend their time; after the work of the day , my friend enjoys the outside even more by sitting on a jetty and chatting with a mate about the day that's just passed and anything else that comes up. They spend this time, what he calls 'jetty time', sitting between the glittering stars and their sparkling reflection on the water: the natural world becomes the space for conversation and friendship after a long day of adventure and fun.

Finally, engage with the gift of creation by seeing how the Bible weaves experience of nature into its words of truth and life. Jesus used images of creation to teach his disciples and transform their perspective. In Luke 12:22–34, he invites the disciples to look at birds and flowers: look, Jesus says, at God's care displayed abundantly and wildly all over creation. See that fragile flower? It's beautiful, and that's because God made it. He made you too, and makes you beautiful just the same. See that bird calling over the salt marshes? It's full up and happy – and, just like that bird, you too will receive what food you need straight from the hand of God. Learn from this world and see that God is God, and God is good, and you are always, *always* held.

An image of creation from the Bible underlies the whole of this book too – Jeremiah 17:7–8's 'tree planted by the water' is the image we're using to talk about how we grow as Christians living in God's grace. Nature can thus become an expression of hopes, prayers and identities, a vessel for something rich and full and life-giving. I hope you've seen that in this chapter as we've gently explored experiences of creation, right from sunsets to salt marshes to starfish to leaves. Let's return once more to that beach where it all began.

You see, it's not a waste of your time to watch a starfish slowly descending into the foam of the waves. It's time well spent – thankful time; 'awe time'; time of discovery and grace. Crouch between the rocks and feel the cool water rising around your legs as the tide comes in, as the tide comes in and bears away the bright orange starfish out into the sea.

Headphones time

As before, here are some questions and ideas to help you think and pray through this chapter. Use them as you will – or grab a friend and get outside! Enjoy the world God's given us and learn to see him through it: the heavens proclaim the glory of God and the skies display the work of his hands.

- Have you ever felt the presence of God as you've spent time in creation? Where were you, and how did (and how does) this encounter help you to know God?

- What is one thing you want to try and do to learn to see God through creation? Choose one thing, whether it's an idea from this chapter or something you've thought of yourself, and aim to give it a go in the next couple of weeks.

- How can knowing that God reveals himself through creation help you to share God's love with those who don't know him yet?

- Look up Gerard Manley Hopkins' poem 'As Kingfishers Catch Fire' and spend some time reading it and reflecting on its words. It might seem difficult to understand at first, but there's beautiful meaning in there about how God's grace plays sweet music all through the created world.

- 'He also made the stars': these five words appear in the creation account in Genesis. They're easy to skim over – but as you read Genesis 1 and enjoy the poetry describing God's creative work, try to pause as you read and give thanks to God. They are incredible words describing an incredible Creator!

Soundtrack

'Planet Earth II suite' by Hans Zimmer.

This is the theme tune to the BBC's *Planet Earth II* series and it is fantastic. As my sister says, this music just makes you think of big things – the big-ness of this whole created planet.

Story stop: Summer camp songs

Here's the third of our story stops. I'm maybe ten or eleven here – an age at which peace and quiet often don't exist! Yet this memory is one in which I start to learn that quietness and silence are really valuable, a lesson that I still struggle to remember. Think about times in your life when silence and quiet have been significant. What was good about it, and why?

― ― ― ― ― ▪ ▪ ▪ ― ― ―

Hyper voices echo across the starlit courtyard as we run, excited to be on summer camp and up later than our parents would usually allow. Our wonderful leaders smile tiredly and shepherd us towards the dining room, where steaming cups of marshmallowy hot chocolate await. We chatter loudly as we queue up, comparing the friendship bracelets we've made, or the smudges of face paint still visible from the team challenge. We relive again and again the most exciting moments of the day.

The room slowly quietens as one by one we sit down to enjoy our mugs of chocolatey goodness, spoons scraping the sides for any elusive morsels of sticky marshmallow. Our dorm leaders ask us how our days have been as they subtly pass out sheets of song lyrics, and, in time, a guitar starts to play somewhere in the room. Young ears pause to listen and voices start to pick up the tune; we smile across the tables at each other as we sing. Excitement settles to contentment and our hearts begin to beat in time as we sing of the love God has for us.

Peace descends; the memories of the day rest holy in the quiet space created for them. We realise we're at home in the story God sings over, around and through us.

When the last dregs of hot chocolate are drained from their cups, we are led out of the dining room towards our beds. We go quietly, more sleepily, one dorm at a time, with only an occasional stray whisperer grinning at their friends. We cross the courtyard and the silent stars sparkle down at us, the night air warm and our hyper voices quelled for the evening. The silence is palpable, tangible and real – not representing a lack of excitement but instead filling the space with peace.

We pull on pyjamas and settle into bed – and although there are the usual giggles and secret codes knocked on furniture across the room, the sense of that quiet stays with us. God's presence is near.

Those nights on camp are some of my most precious memories. Silence is not a lack of noise; it is a positive thing in itself that can speak to us wordlessly and powerfully. Rest from the chatter of life is key – and this is what we'll look at more in the next chapter.

8

So what actually is 'quiet time'?

Learning to hear God in the silence

Though silence sometimes involves the absence of speech, it always involves the act of listening.[56]

Silence: a sound we often don't hear. I sit in Costa writing these words – I can hear happy music playing through the sound system while the coffee machines shlurp and thud; I can hear chattering voices, rustling newspapers, loud children and their exasperated mums, the jingle of change passing hands in exchange for cake. As I walk home, I'll probably put my headphones in and turn the music up loud (pretending I'm in a movie with an epic soundtrack); at home, there'll be lots of laughs and conversations and noise because my cousins are staying for the week and every day's a party when they're here. It's fun and crazy and really non-stop and, particularly as an extrovert, I love it.

So, in the midst of all this, what good could silence possibly be? What space is there for it? I don't know if you have much space for silence and quietness in your life – maybe you do, but I'd guess that actually most of us fill up the silent spaces with distraction and sound. Why should we make the effort to love the silence when we have Netflix at our fingertips?

Despite all of this, I know deep down that quiet spaces are really valuable – even for an extrovert. Like in the previous story stop, I know that quiet spaces can become moments full of peace, truth and gentleness, places where we can know that God is near and where we can find ourselves in him. We have to learn to love the silence even though it costs us more effort than distracting ourselves with easier things to think about.

My trip to the little monastery in Assisi taught me much about the value of silence and quiet. Every night, we came together in the cool stone crypt of the monastery's chapel to say Compline (night prayer) in English; as part of this service, Jamie, the Dean of Clare College, would share a few words of wisdom.

It was either the first or second evening that Jamie spoke about the value of silence. Silence is not a lack of noise, he said, but a positive and full thing in itself. It's the place where words overflow; it's what you get when the words don't work any more, when the words run out.

I was stunned – it was one of those moments where words spoken by someone else hit you right in the middle when you're least expecting it. *Maybe silence is something I need*, I thought. *Maybe these five days in Assisi need to be a time of putting aside the noise and letting the words run out, letting them overflow into the full space of quiet and waiting.*

Letting the words run out is a tricky thing when you're an extroverted writer whose go-to ways of praying, processing and thinking are either to put pen to paper or to gather with friends and chat until late. Yet something inside of me was absolutely certain that this Assisi week needed to be about letting my pen fall still and my evenings fall quiet. I needed to stop crowding the silent spaces with my own words and thoughts, and instead let the silence swell into wordless meaning; I needed to stop distracting myself and in the quiet spaces be led to confront the things that I'd been ignoring. I needed to face the music by embracing the silence.

So, after that Compline time, I walked purposefully across the grass outside the crypt and sat cross-legged on the gravelly wall overlooking the valley. The sun was setting and the valley was alight with a golden glow; the dome of the Porziuncola stood out in the skyline, shining dully orange. I took off my watch and put it to the side with my Bible. I'd stay here until the first star came out, and I'd be silent; I'd follow God into the quiet place. I was more than a little bit apprehensive!

It can be scary to be silent. When you strip away noise and distraction, all that's left is you, the wide sky and the voice of God. What will you find as you listen? Who is residing at the centre of your heart? As you search, hand in hand with God, you pray and hope and question and wait. What is it that God wants me to hear?

It's a bit like these words from Psalm 139:23–24: 'Search me, O God, and know my heart: test me and know my anxious thoughts. See if there is any offensive way in me, and lead me in the way everlasting.'

> God, I'm here with empty hands and I'm an open book in front of you: you can see all of the things that are confusing me and tying me in knots; you can see all the things that bring me joy; you can see everything that I think and believe about you and me and this world. Help me to see with your eyes, and send me out to live with your new vision and purpose.

This is what I prayed each night as I sat on that monastery wall, looking to everyone else like I was doing nothing, but knowing for myself that this was an important thing to be doing. After the first little while of quiet, accompanied only by cicadas chirping and distant dogs barking, I found myself relaxing and resting, learning to trust that to be known and searched and challenged by God is a good thing. Even if he was confronting me about something that was really hard for me to think about, I knew that it was okay. He is a kind God, and in the silent space he taught me to hold the weight of quietness in my hands as I waited and rested patiently for his timing to be full, for his voice to speak life and truth into every feeling and situation.

Because I think that's often it – prayer is often about learning to wait for the right time, the time when God chooses to speak. An image Jamie used in another Assisi Compline was that of a kingfisher: prayer is sometimes about waiting for an hour until you suddenly see sunlight flash off a kingfisher's wing for a second. Prayer is sometimes the long wait for a sudden flash of realisation, a glimpse of the 'movement of a curtain',[57] it is sometimes the walk on the Emmaus road that ends startlingly with a moment of recognition as Jesus breaks open the bread. (See Luke 24:13–35 for the full Emmaus story.)

Silence and quietness can help you as you wait for God to speak, as you hold out for the kingfisher to flit into view. This doesn't mean that every time you spend with God has to be quiet. Greater quietness does not equal greater spirituality or connection with God – which I think is the mistake we sometimes make in using the name 'quiet time' when we talk about prayer. Prayer can be shouted or sung or spoken or whispered or laughed or cried – or it can be silent. Silence and quietness are tools to help you grow roots in God's grace, and they can be more useful at some times than at others.

Why not try it for yourself? Put aside an hour this week to go and sit in a place where you'll not be disturbed. Just sit in the quiet and ask God to help you to wait for him and listen to what he has to say. Lay out before him all the things that your hands have been holding – everything that you've been thinking about, whether it's worrying you or making you feel really joy-full, and just sit with the feelings that rise to the surface. Give God the opportunity to speak in his timing and in his way – and don't worry if you fidget, or find your mind wandering! This is all part of the process, and maybe it's what Jesus meant when he said to his disciples: 'When you pray, go into your room, close the door and pray to your Father, who is unseen. Then your Father, who sees what is done in secret, will reward you' (Matthew 6:6).

I hope you'll find the silence worth it – I know I have at several different times. In Assisi, God taught me in the silence that he loves me no matter what; that he heals wounds when you give him permission to; that day-by-day he is making me new. Years ago, in another time of silence, God showed me how to begin letting go of everyday worry and stress and instead just breathe in his grace. Sometimes I've not heard anything when I've sat in silence – yet I've always found that practising dwelling in that listening space is always worth it. What will you discover?

Silence is also not just for when you're alone, even though we've only spoken about it in the context of private prayer and 'quiet time' so far. Some of my most precious moments of silence and quiet have been experienced with other people.

One such moment occurred on my last evening as co-leader of my college Christian Union. We had a time of prayer, praying 'thank you's for the previous year and boldness for the new leaders over the following year. Everyone had prayed; we sat around a table laden with bunches of thank-you flowers and the remnants of a pizza feast. We waited to see if anyone else wanted to pray something out loud before we said the definitive 'Amen'.

We waited and no one spoke. A tangible silence enveloped the room, a surprising peace resting over all of us sitting there with our eyes closed and tummies full of celebration food. There was a wordless feeling, bringing us together in peace and unity – until someone began to giggle because of how long we'd been silent. One of the new leaders said the final 'Amen' and we relaxed, transformed by that short moment of deep, quiet peace. I just remember one of the guys saying: 'That silence wasn't awkward for me; it was amazing. I don't know how to describe it – but it was good.'

In such random moments of collective silence, the Spirit of God speaks. God chooses to build his church through these shared spaces of prayer and quiet; through wordlessness, the Spirit speaks to our hearts in ways that cannot easily be described but which yet have tangible consequences. For us that night at Christian Union, unexpected silence gave us a sense of peace about the handover process: God was showing us that the change in leadership was exactly as he wanted it to be. As one of the outgoing leaders, this gave me great joy and encouragement and peace in the midst of change – and thus we see that God transforms our perspectives, feelings and selves by his grace even if we cannot put words to it. In his grace lies the power of silence and quiet as tools to help us pray and be transformed to live by his truth, whether this is experienced together or alone.

This strikes at another key point I've experienced about silence: it is often in the midst of change or struggle or really busy times that God calls me to sit quietly with him. At my busiest, most restless moments, he asks me to be still and rest – it's counterintuitive but it's true, and being still is probably one of the most helpful things he could invite me to do when I'm running around trying to keep the world spinning. I have a definite tendency to bite off more than I can chew and God, through encouraging me strongly to rest, is always teaching me that he's the one who keeps this blue marble of a planet spinning – not me!

One story about Jesus that I really love is when he falls asleep in a boat, right in the middle of a storm. Jesus has been travelling around teaching crowds about God's kingdom. The day turns to dusk and then to dark; the disciples take Jesus on a boat, just as he was, to the other side of a lake. (You'll find where I'm reading this from in Mark 4:35–41.) That phrase, 'just as he was', is an interesting one in the original Greek text – no one knows precisely what it means. Perhaps it's suggesting that Jesus is worn out and tired; this is supported by him falling asleep on a cushion in the stern even as waves start to rush in and swamp the boat. (As a side note, the Greek word for cushion is one of my favourites: it's *proskephalē*, and it literally means 'the thing towards the head'.)

Jesus sleeps tight until the disciples shake him awake. 'C'mon Jesus! Don't you care if we drown?!'

Jesus calmly stands up, rubs his tired eyes and speaks out to the storm: 'Be muzzled, stop your growling. Be still.'

The waves hear Jesus' voice and cease their movement; the wind dies down. The disciples quake in their sandals and Jesus looks them sternly in the eye: 'Where was your faith?'

So much about Jesus is revealed in this short story. Read and dwell on it; who is Jesus in this passage? Most recently, my answer to this question has been that Jesus is our example of entering into rest and quiet space, even in the midst of busyness and stormy times.

He's travelled and taught all day and, at the end of it, all he needs is rest. His head hits the pillow in the stern of the boat and he gives no more thought to his safety or his disciples' comfort – it's like he knows implicitly that he can sleep because God is always watching over them to protect them and because, of course, he is Jesus and he can still the storm.

It's the disciples who didn't have this faith to be quiet and rest, even though they literally had God sleeping in the stern of their boat. I reckon they'd be shouting loudly as they swept water into buckets to throw back into the sea; as they worked through the night to keep themselves afloat you'd be able to hear their voices get more and more panicky as you stood on the shore of Lake Galilee.

This is because they didn't recognise who Jesus was – they didn't see him clearly enough to know that he was the Messiah, mighty to save. It's only in Mark 8 that we get Peter's confession that Jesus is the Christ (and even then, he misunderstands what this means); at this point, the disciples couldn't rest easy in the boat because they didn't know the power that was with them and the power that was watching over them.

Jesus is our example of how to trust God and enter into the full resting space of silence and quiet. We can fall asleep at night because we can trust that God never slumbers; we can sit for an hour in silence because we know that we can leave aside our other jobs and have empty hands for a little while. There's no place else we need to be if we're in the place that God has called us to – even if that place seems counterintuitive and counterproductive.

So truly quiet 'quiet time' is an amazing way to grow roots in God's grace because it allows us to let go of the belief that we need to strive to be strong enough to save ourselves, and instead it teaches us that all we need to do is fall into the palm of God's hand. (Do you remember Rachel's words from earlier?) We can rest within our busy times and be quiet within our noisy times – and enter into the often-wordless mystery of the vast expanse of God's grace to be refreshed and renewed and set back on the right track.

Renewal and refreshment are indeed what we most often find in God's silent space; he takes our prayers and renews our perspectives, giving us new purposes. Time spent in quietness prepares us for the rest of the day, for the good works he has prepared for us to do. The quiet space emboldens us to walk through the noise and bring God's kingdom to it. The roots we grow in God's grace cause us to bear fruit for God's glory and others' blessing.

Silence, quiet and rest are thus about letting go of our small views of God, small views which tell us that we have to hold on to our faith by our fingertips and keep bucketing water out of the boat ourselves – because God *surely* isn't big enough to give us all we need, and *surely* isn't powerful enough to still the storms.

In the quiet space, we allow our views to be expanded so that they embrace the inexplicable about God: that he is inconceivably good, powerful and loving – and that he is all of these to measures beyond our imagination. Our perspectives widen; the frame of the porthole through which we've been gazing at God buckles and breaks and the ocean rushes in. We come to deeply know that God is like an expansive, starry ocean, vast enough to provide for all our needs;

powerful enough to still any storm; beautiful enough to amaze us for eternity.

This is the true 'quiet time': trusting that God is so great that we can take time to rest, to enter the silence amid the storm and to be transformed from the inside out by God's vision, grace and truth.

Headphones time

Here, the headphones analogy is perhaps the most apt it has ever been: put some headphones in; block out all the other distracting noises; spend some time dwelling on what you've read as you listen to God.

- What's the one big thing you've taken away from this chapter about how you can spend time with God?

- Read Psalm 46. What stands out to you about the circumstances in which God asks us to 'Be still, and know that I am God' (v. 10)? How does acknowledging who God is help you to stop in the midst of busy times, rest and enter the silent spaces?

- How does thinking about silence make you feel? Are you afraid of what you might find in the quiet places, or are you excited to rest and listen to God in this way? Take these feelings to God and ask him to show you what the most helpful way is for you to use silence and quiet to listen to him. Perhaps read Psalm 139 and reflect on how God sees you: does this take away the fear of what God might show you about yourself?

- Do you usually think of silence as a tool to help you pray? If it would be useful for you, what could you do in your life to create more space for quiet and silence?

• A friend once told me about a silent Christian Union committee meeting: intentionally, no one spoke; everyone stayed silent, praying and listening for God's voice. Are you involved in any groups where having a silent meeting could be something good (and fun) to try?

Soundtrack

'Be still for the presence of the Lord' by David Evans.

This song kept popping into my head when we visited churches in Assisi – its lyrics invite us to step into the holy ground of silent spaces. Listen: what encourages you to take some 'quiet time' in order to listen to God?

9

Keeping Christ's word central

Seeking God through church worship

God does not need our worship. We worship to enlarge our sense of the holy, so that we can feel and know the presence of the Lord, who is with us always.[58]

The next two chapters are going to be all about one small word that contains a huge amount of meaning: church.

Church: the place where we gather, hungry to hear God's word and bring our prayers to him together. The radical community built on relationships that cross all borders and boundaries. A place where difficult and painful conflict can and should be confronted with God's truth and intentional peace-making. The beautiful yet imperfect vessel of God's glory on the earth, purposed to love mercy, act justly and walk humbly with our God, however much bravery this calls us to have. Diverse unity; boundless love; risky faith. Encouragement and honesty held in a safe space of community and family.

These are just a few phrases that spring to my mind when I think about what church is or could be to me. Take a few moments to scribble in the margins any phrases and words that occur to you about your experience and perception of church.

Colossians 3:15–16 is part of Paul's instruction to the church in Colossae about how they can live as a holy community of God's people. Our reflection on church will have its roots in these words. This chapter will focus on verse 16 and church in terms of liturgy (the formal patterns of worship in church services, the 'order of service' if you like). The next chapter will look at verse 15 and how church is a family and a community described as 'one body'. Both chapters will ask the question: how can these aspects of church help us to be rooted in God's grace?

Here are the Colossians verses for you to read before we begin:

> Let the peace of Christ rule in your hearts, since as members of one body you were called to peace. And be thankful. Let the message of Christ dwell among you richly as you teach and admonish one another with all wisdom through psalms, hymns and songs from the Spirit, singing to God with gratitude in your hearts.

Pray that God would give you his eyes to see church as he sees it, no matter what your previous experiences of church have been.

'Let the message of Christ dwell among you richly', verse 16 beautifully begins. Let Christ's life-giving, grace-full truth mould you and shape you; let it dwell inside you and transform you from the inside out. 'You' is plural: let the word of Christ dwell in *all of you*, all of you collectively, together as one church made up of many people. As you all sit there in those church pews or seats, meet with God as you hear Jesus' words and let them take root in your hearts; let them grow you into trees planted by water that send out their roots by the stream. Let your spirits be touched by God's Spirit as you come together to respond to him, turning your faces towards the light.

This is a beautiful picture – but it's often not our predominant attitude as we go to church services. Even if the word of God is being preached faithfully (and sometimes it's not); even if the songs we sing are saturated with biblical words (and sometimes they're not); even if we are completely surrounded by the word of Christ – we often don't have ears to hear it or hearts to let it in. Our minds wander and we find ourselves thinking more about the ladybird crawling across the shoulder of the person in front of us, or how tired the preacher looks or how loud the person behind us sings. We often don't give the word of Christ a chance to dwell in us richly at church – whether this is on an individual level as our minds wander, or on a collective level because the word of God isn't kept as the central focus of our time together. (We'll talk more about this later.)

The all-too-familiar problem of our minds wandering at church was humorously described by Arthur (one of my university supervisors) as he preached in college chapel:

> All too often I stand in my pew and, as we sing a hymn I think less about the words than the hairstyle of the person in front of me; how my own head looks from the back; how cool my wicked American accent sounds when I sing...

He grinned and reflected further:

> I think about all of these things when really, church is about submitting to God's truth. It's not about how good we sound when we sing or how great our hair looks, but about us being underneath the word of God, submitting to and pursuing truth.

These aren't his exact words, but they capture the sense of his sermon – and they capture the sense of Paul's words to the Colossians as he encourages them to 'let the message of Christ dwell among you richly'.

Let the word of Christ dwell in you richly: may hearing his words be your priority when you walk into that church. Whatever you expect your experience of the church service to be, whether you expect to listen to a familiar message for the 50th time or learn something totally new about God's grace; whether you feel like you'll experience God miraculously or instead just simply wait in his presence searchingly; whether you hope to hear from God through spending time singing worship with others or think you'll find yourself pacing the back hall with a wriggly child – whatever your expectation or experience of church liturgy, enter church with a heart ready to receive.

Enter church with a heart ready to receive; prepare your heart before you go. Find ways that help you to get ready to enter that church space of together-worship – try extending your walk to church so that you have more time to steady your thoughts and pray; perhaps look up the Bible passages in advance so you can get familiar with them before hearing them from the front. Get to church early: don't leave it till the last few seconds before you slide into your seat: get there in time to see the room fill up with God's people and his presence. I understand that these suggestions aren't always practical, but if you're struggling with receiving God's grace in church services, why not make space to give them a go?

Enter church with a heart ready to receive, arms wide open to the mercy of Jesus Christ. Be ready to listen to God both in the post-service conversation over coffee or wine and in the formal time of prayers, sung worship and sermon. Be open to him whether you sit in the front pew or pace the back hall. The whole time from when you enter that door to when you leave is a time where patterns of grace and pursuing God might be practised and encountered in community – and this is a real blessing.

It's a blessing because to pursue God together is massively encouraging. When you get to the end of a long week and just want to bury your head under the duvet and ignore the world, *go to church anyway*. There's nothing like it for helping you to refocus your perspective on the grace of God and get ready for the week ahead. There's nothing like it for being challenged and stretched in your faith, for growing in wisdom and gratefulness to God, for being comforted in times of struggle.

I experienced this one summer when I went to visit some friends in London for a weekend. A few weeks before, I had decided to stop

Keeping Christ's word central 125

going to the church I'd been going to at home because, at that time, I felt that for me to go there would be more faith-frustrating than faith-building.

When I got to London, I hadn't been to church for about four weeks. On Sunday morning, I made pancakes with Leah at her house and then we drove to church. Entering, I felt such great joy at being welcomed into Leah's church. It was wonderful to be able to sing worship songs and listen to a Bible talk and pray and *do all of these things together*. There was something about seeking God *together* that totally refreshed me, something that I'd missed when I'd been away from church and seeking God alone.

And I think this is partly why Paul wrote to the *whole* church in Colossae, using the plural 'you'. He says, 'Let the message of Christ dwell among you richly'; let it dwell in *all of you* as you meet together. Work together to make God's word central to your church gatherings because *together* is so much better than *alone* – in fact, *together* is the pattern and life we were made for.

We see this so clearly when we look at God himself: God is Father, Spirit and Son; God *is* relationship and togetherness, he *is* love embodied in triune community. When Jesus died for us, he invited us into this deep community: 'We, made in his image, are beckoned forth into this divine participation'[59] – and this is amazing.

We practise this amazing gift of participation both when we spend time with God alone and when we come together as church and proclaim our faith in Jesus. We embody the words Jesus prayed for all his followers: 'I am in them and you are in me. May they experience such perfect unity that the world will know that you sent me and that you love them as much as you love me' (John 17:23, NLT).

Let the word of Christ dwell in us richly, shaping and forming our church meetings and communities. As we dwell in this richness, the richness of the gospel, we cannot but experience and embody the unity and love that exists between Jesus and God the Father. Through our collective times of worship, God's kingdom comes as a kingdom that is a community and a family, not just a random collection of individuals who don't really know each other. We are brought together in unity and community, and this is what makes us distinctive in a world of individualism and pride.

Therefore, letting Christ's word dwell richly in our churches is so important. It builds God's kingdom, both as we 'dwell' individually, entering church with an open-hearted attitude, and as we 'dwell' collectively, putting Jesus intentionally and always at the centre of our church worship. Our liturgy, orders of services and church rhythms and practices must have at their core the grace of Jesus.

It breaks my heart that there are churches that don't keep Jesus' words central. I don't know what your experience of church has been. Have you always been involved in churches where Jesus' name is the only name, where the word of God is the foundational and authoritative voice? If so – that's amazing, and I am so full of joy for you and your church.

If not – I am deeply sorry, and saddened with you. I am sorry if you've been to churches that have, unintentionally or otherwise, used the word of God to hurt you. I'm sorry if you've had an encounter with God's family that has left you reeling and reaching frantically for anything solid to keep you above the waves.

I know how it feels, and it hurts. Yet, have hope and keep the faith. Pray and look for a church where the Bible is taught faithfully, where grace is the heartbeat, where freedom reigns and love abounds. There are churches out there that are like this; God is always raising up people to follow him and lead his church servant-heartedly. God always hears our desperate prayers for his church to grow in grace and truth and integrity. He hears our prayers for love, acceptance and unity.

So, I really have just one thing to say about the liturgy of our church services: it must communicate the word of Christ faithfully, and that is all. Liturgy, the patterns of formal worship and prayer, can look different from church to church, tradition to tradition, generation to generation – but it *must* communicate Christ's words of love, freedom and truth. It must help us to trust God and put our roots down in his grace.

Growing up, I went to churches that all followed a similar pattern of service. They were led, prayed and preached from the front, with a handful of songs and maybe an interactive drama or children's activity for everyone to join in with throughout the service. This was normal for me, for church to be informal and to be about a balance between listening and joining in, with a coffee-and-chat time at the end. (My parents would inevitably stay super long at this part when my sister and I wanted to go home!)

When I started at Clare College, Cambridge, I was totally unused to and even slightly dismissive of the formal, 'high-church' style of worship practised in our college chapel. I sat wearing my gown (I know, very Hogwarts!) with the rest of my year group at the welcome service, and was totally amazed by the response that such a service received. Despite, or perhaps because of, its formality – it involved lots of sitting down and standing up as the choir sang choral music,[60] and some reading out of set prayers from the orders of service – the service really engaged with this group of 150 nervous 18-year-olds. It provided a subtly God-focused, curiosity-awakening and welcoming service that didn't feel too weird to those who hadn't been to church before.

My perception of what 'good' church liturgy was changed as I experienced that welcome service and all of the future, equally beautiful services in chapel. At weekday Evensong, we'd hear a couple of Bible readings, say the creed together and hear the choir sing the Magnificat (Mary's song in Luke 1:46–55), the Nunc Dimittis (Simeon's song in Luke 2:29–32) and some psalms. The psalms form the core of chapel services, as they have done for centuries. In chapel, I also learned the value of the seasons of the Christian year,[61] including Advent and Lent; I went to my first ever Ash Wednesday service at chapel and was again amazed by the richness of the worship through the more liturgical, formal pattern that was unlike anything I'd experienced before going to university.

At that Ash Wednesday service, I sat next to Claire and we enjoyed the service together. I read the Bible reading from the lectern, in front of all those people; I listened to Jamie give the sermon and heard God's grace in words I never could've come up with myself. We lined up for the 'imposition of the ashes' – later, I wrote these words in a blog post:

> As the first notes of the Miserere[62] soared, the Dean of Clare College… smudged ash cruciform on my head, murmured the words (I think they were these): 'Remember that you are dust, and to dust you shall return. Turn away from sin and be faithful to Christ.'

> I am dust, and to dust I shall return. I am fragile and mortal. The ash on my forehead calls me to remember and to repent, to turn in my weakness and – here is the stunning part – to know that Jesus forgives me my weakness and sin and strengthens my steps as I go. Jesus makes me new.[63]

This is what worshipping *together* means – it's reminding each other again and again of the grace of Christ. Can we know this grace *both* by joining in with kids' action songs *and* by listening to beautiful Latin choral music? Can we draw close to God *both* by listening to one person read prayers from the front *and* by reciting the creed in unison in a little college chapel?

'Yes!' is the resounding answer. Jesus dwells in all church services that keep his word central, whether that happens through the liturgy of formal chapel services or the pattern of something more informal.

He's with his church when they adopt a café-style approach: sitting around tables eating doughnuts while the kids do some colouring and someone speaks from the front. He's with us however we gather and encourage each other with his truth – in fact, 'we need not be overly concerned with the question of the correct form for worship... Nowhere does the New Testament prescribe a particular form for worship.'[64] We have freedom to be with God in any way that truly enhances our experience of the word of Christ dwelling in us richly.

Perhaps you'd never stopped to consider this before and have always been to churches that have similar styles or patterns of worship. Now is your time to think about it: is the way you're worshipping at church the most helpful for you and those around you? If your general answer to this question is no, think specifically. Why is it not the most helpful for you? Is it because you're entering church reluctantly, with a heart closed rather than open? Or is it because the way your church community worships does not keep Christ's word at the centre? Or is it because you or those around you just don't 'click' with that style of worship? Or do you have another reason?

All of these questions can be good questions to ponder. In response to your pondering, you could challenge yourself to enter church openly each week, taking the time to prepare yourself before you go. You could challenge your church to think about how it worships and what its focus is in worship. Challenge both yourself and your church to try out different forms of worship and liturgy, to see if different people 'click' with different styles. Above all, be led in your pondering and challenging by Christ's word and God's Spirit: it is his love that we're seeking to respond to in our church services.

A few final words on the nature of liturgy and worship come from Jamie who, for BBC Radio 4's *Sunday Worship*, spoke about the relationship between liturgy and theatre, comparing liturgical celebrations of church services to performances of the stage. The movements of church services, which for Jamie involve the more formal components of college chapel services, are like theatrical performances in which the whole cast acts in relation to the one principal actor: Christ. This all goes to communicate that:

> God is really interested in this particular bit of your story. God's particularly interested in how your story fits with the overarching narrative of salvation and of glory and it's the glory of the human being fully alive in Christ in which we see the action of God working most extraordinarily.[65]

Our together-worship in church services, whatever that looks like for each of us, should always be for this purpose: to communicate to each other and receive from God the message that he is interested in us; that we fit into the story of salvation; that we're called to be alive in Christ; that this calling is extraordinary.

Headphones time

Here are some questions to help you to think and pray through what it means to seek God together.

- Spend some time reading and reflecting on Colossians 3:16 again. How could you be praying this for the church community you're a part of?

- Think about your own experiences of church, both past and present. Are you at a church that keeps Jesus' words central to its worship and liturgy? If not – how could you challenge your church to refocus and 'let Christ's message dwell among you richly'?

- Look up Rublev's icon 'Trinity'. Notice the direction in which each figure is looking as you reflect and pray about how God invites you into relationship with him. Maybe read John 17:6–11. What amazes you about what Jesus prays here?

- Are there different styles of church worship that you might want to experience? For example, a café-style service, the sung worship of Taizé, a more informal 'loud-music-worship-concert' gathering, a more restful 'high-church' liturgy? Find out where you could go to worship God in these different ways; pray that he would guide you as you seek him.

- People often turn to Acts 2:42–47 to reflect on what church is. How does this passage challenge and encourage you in your thoughts about church community and worship? How could this description speak into and shape how we develop and grow as church?

Soundtrack

'Overflow' by Tenth Avenue North.

How does this song capture the essence of what it means to worship God together?

Story stop: Church search

This is our final story stop, and this time the story is taken from the very beginning of my second year of university when I was newly discovering how family can be found in church. What are your experiences of church? Are they mostly positive or negative, or a mix of both?

Mike Pilavachi, leader of Soul Survivor and guest preacher at Holy Trinity, finished his sermon and invited people to take some time to pray and be in God's presence. Music started to play; some of the congregation stood to join in with the song. I sat and stared down at my hands, willing my eyes not to fill with tears and wondering why the tears were coming anyway.

Next to me was a first-year student from my college who I had only recently met. I was with her as part of our 'church search' breakfast: an event where older students take first years to different churches so they can find a place to settle. I was meant to be looking after this student – not crying!

Even more annoying to me was the fact that I don't usually get super emotional and start crying in church. It had never happened before, and I didn't really know why it was happening now. I wanted to take back the tears that had started to fall and pull myself together – especially in front of this girl I didn't really know, and especially as I was in a church that I'd never really been to before.

Yet something, somehow, was not letting me stop the tears from falling. Inside me, there was something breaking and shifting. There was a feeling welling up that I did not have words for. In retrospect, after nearly a year of praying through this feeling, I'd say it felt a bit like this verse from Isaiah 43:19: 'See, I am doing a new thing! Now it springs up; do you not perceive it? I am making a way in the wilderness and streams in the wasteland.' At the time, I did not have this perspective – only tears and wordlessness and a first year sitting next to me whom I was supposed to be welcoming to church. Instead, I was uncharacteristically crying! It was such a surprise to me when this first year, Tanya, put her arm around me and started to pray for me. She prayed peace for me, and comfort.

When my eyes were finally dry, Tanya and I joined in the worship songs going on around us. God was near – and I knew then that this church was a safe place, a place where it was okay not to be okay and where people, however little you knew them, would be sensitive to your hurt and pray if you needed it. This is church: a place where our weakness can be shown so that God's victory can come and strengthen us and change us.

─────────── ▪ ▪ ▪ ───────────

I moved to Holy Trinity a couple of weeks later and have found there what so many find in churches all across the world: the love of God shown through the people he has made his own. It's something so precious and something that's also often missed; in the next chapter, we'll be asking the question of how we can be rooted in God's grace through our church communities, and what to do when this is tricky.

10

Letting the peace of Christ rule

Living God's grace in our church communities

As family we go.[66]

If the phrase for the last chapter was 'Let the word of Christ dwell in you richly', the phrase for this chapter is 'Let the peace of Christ rule in your hearts'. It's from that key Colossians verse, 3:15: 'Let the peace of Christ rule in your hearts, since as members of one body you were called to peace. And be thankful.'

These are the words we'll use to explore church community. We've looked at liturgy and forms of church worship – and now we'll dig deeper to see how we can become rooted in God's grace through being part of God's family, through being built up together as one faithful body. Liturgy is a part of this; now let's look at the whole.

'Let the peace of Christ rule in your hearts', verse 15 beautifully begins. Let peace rule, peace here meaning 'more than a feeling of tranquillity. It means unity, wholesomeness and health.'[67] In this context, peace is outward-looking rather than introspective; it exists *between* individuals, binding and joining them together as a unified community.

Let peace rule: be joined together and let wholeness define your community, not just your individual self. May Christ's peace be your defining feature and way of life. Be tied together in Jesus: may peace rule in your hearts (remembering that 'your' is plural).

What does this mean? What does it mean on an average weekday or Sunday morning that God has called his people to peace, wholeness and unity with one another? To answer this question, we're going to explore three images for what church community is: a body, a dwelling-place for God and a shelter.

Church as a body

Colossians 3:15 continues, 'Since as members of one body you were called to peace.' *Members of one body* is what Paul calls the individuals who make up the church community, those who have been called to peace in all its fullness. This is his metaphor for wholeness, togetherness and unity under Christ – can you think of other places where Paul uses this same picture?

We find this 'body language' scattered throughout Paul's letters; he longs, deeply and often painfully, for unity and peace to rule in the Christian community. Where there is division, he calls for people to refocus on Christ and love each other. Where there is disorderliness in church services, he reminds people that God creates order and has called his community to peace.

This is clearly the case in Paul's first letter to the Corinthians. The Corinthian church was in a messy state – Paul had received reports (1:11; 16:17) that they were splitting into factions (1:12); that sexual immorality was happening and was not being dealt with properly (6—7); that church services, worship and the taking of the Lord's supper were chaotic, unfair and unclear (10:14–11:34).

Chapter 12 discusses this last point through the issue of spiritual gifts. The Corinthians had begun to value some gifts more than others; they valued some people in their church more than others for possessing the 'greater' gifts. It's this attitude of partiality and arrogance that underlies the Corinthian problem. To confront it, Paul uses 'body language': the metaphor of many parts joined together to form one body. Read 1 Corinthians 12:12–27 to see just how he does this.

Do you see? God's church is *one* body in which each person is valued equally for the gifts, strengths and talents they bring to the community: 'God has placed the parts in the body, every one of them, just as he wanted them to be' (v. 18). If you're good at preaching, go and preach (and if you're a woman who's heard that you can't preach because you're a woman, go and preach anyway).[68] If you're good at encouraging people, go and encourage. If you're good at listening to people, go and listen. If you're good at admin, go and administrate – organise the church! But don't step on someone else's toes by saying that your strengths are better and more valuable than theirs or by trying to do their job for them. Lift each other up in love, for this is what Jesus has done for you. Be humble; let peace rule in your hearts as you seek to serve God and each other.

This view that everyone is equal and precious in God's kingdom and community unlocks so much freedom for us as we pursue God together. When we learn to work together and encourage each other in our gifts, we become much more of a welcoming, effective community. We reflect God's unconditional love in a far brighter way. We allow each other to thrive in his grace and bear fruit for his glory, helping each other to put down deep roots instead of competing to be 'the best Christian'. Let's stop competing; we have far greater things to be doing. Let's seek his kingdom, together.

The question is: how can we put this 'body language' into practice?

First, think about your own strengths and gifts. You might already know what it is you're good at and what your strengths are – gifts and strengths tend to show themselves naturally through our personalities and actions. Listen to what others praise you for and ask yourself if they speak accurately of who you are and what you're good at.

There are more analytical ways that you can discover your strengths as well. StrengthsFinder[69] is something I did when I was 15 and taking part in Share Jesus International's FRESH leadership course. It's a series of questions which reveal what your top five strengths are. There's a book that goes hand-in-hand with the 'test' to show you what these strengths mean and how you can use them in your work and life – the test costs the price of the book and is well worth it, particularly if you're thinking about leadership roles.

A free and online 'test' you can do can be found here: www. spiritualgiftstest.com. This is something I did in a small group at church, discussing with others how we felt about the gifts it said we had and praying for each other to be both wise and courageous in using and developing the gifts God has given us. Why not gather a group of friends to do something similar?

(Remember to take these 'tests' with a pinch of salt, as they are not always accurate; however, they can give you a very good indication of your different personality traits and strengths.)

Whether you know your specific strengths or not, always encourage each other in serving God. Notice the good things that other people are doing and praise them for it – go and chat to them, leave a note or send a message to say that you've seen the work they're doing and that you're thankful for it. It's right there at the end of Colossians 3:15: 'Be thankful.'

Thankfulness always increases people's confidence and joy. To be seen and noticed, to be known and loved for being who you are and for doing what you do – these are the things which cause you to thrive and grow tall in grace as you see God working in you as you work out your salvation. Be the encouragement for someone else in your church; help them to know that they are seen and valued for being a part of Christ's body.

Finally, always pray. Ask God to help you to see other people's gifts and encourage them. Give thanks that we are all equal members of one body. Pray for peace, humility and wholeness to define your church community, and go do something to make peace abound.

Church as God's dwelling-place

As we learn to value each other as members of one body, we must also always remember that we are members of one *particular* body: Christ's.

Because we are members of Jesus Christ's body, we are incredibly distinctive. In a culture that prioritises individualism and the worship of 'me', it is crazily different to be a part of a community in which everyone looks out for the other person and seeks to put God's will above their own. And it's entirely Jesus who brings this distinction about. Jesus is the one who breathes life, produces holiness and showers joy in our church communities, bringing to us that joined-together peace and wholeness.

Jesus breathes life into his body: just as trees produce seeds which have the potential to become trees of their own, 'so God the Father, by his Holy Spirit, implants in the hearts of some men – those who believe – the very life of Christ, the *LIFE* of God himself'.[70] This life is what awakens people, and those awakened people become the church. Without Christ's life in us, we are nothing. With it, we become the very citizens of the kingdom of God, the very place where God dwells.

Because we are God's dwelling-place, the church is a holy community – a community that grows in righteousness to reflect God's holiness, and live up to the identity that we have been given. The church is the body *of Christ*: how could it strive for anything but holiness in its behaviour? Jesus desires, encourages and produces this holiness in his church. He calls and helps us to live holy. His life is in us.

And because we are God's holy dwelling-place, the church is a place of great joy. Having Jesus' life in us can only produce fearless joy that celebrates both in light and dark – because darkness is as light to him (Psalm 139:11–12). When we meet, we are joy-full as we remind each other of the grace, identity and hope that we have, despite anything else. We are joy-full even under pressure or hardship, because Jesus has set his treasure in jars of clay that we may shine his light.

We are one body, and we are Christ's body. In Jesus, we are distinctive in our life, in our holiness and in our joy. Let's press forwards to live this out in our church communities.

Church as a shelter

Because we are Christ's body, distinctive in all of these ways, we are a shelter and a sanctuary for all. Just as Jesus was inclusive of every single person, so his church, which is his body and his dwelling-place, should also be this radically inclusive. Just as Christ offered his life up for the sake of others, so the church should be generous towards its members and towards those who want to be welcomed in. Just as Jesus desired life in all its fullness for each and every human being, so the church should look to help *all* people grow and thrive, sowing seeds of grace, watering them and praying over them, that each person we encounter – wherever they're from, whoever they are – might trust God, grow roots in his grace and become tall trees bearing good fruit.

Over a fancy college dinner one evening, Jamie (the aforementioned Dean of Clare College) explained his approach to chapel ministry. He said he saw church like a field-hospital[71] – a place into which those with wounds from the world could enter and find healing by encountering God. His prayer for chapel was that each person who came to a service, even if it was only once on a tourist trip to Cambridge, would leave with the sense that church is a place you can go when life throws hard things your way, when trouble hits and you're not quite sure where to turn.

As Christ's body, this is what we can become: the field-hospital and first response team for people who are world-weary and needing rest. Rest is something we all need but rarely get; whether we've been a part of church all of our lives or have never stepped into the sanctuary-place before, we can all benefit from God's gift of rest ministered through his dwelling-place, the church.

I know this because I've experienced it personally so many times. I wrote about one experience in the story stop, and there's another story I'll tell to show you that 'letting the peace of Christ dwell in our hearts' is, at least in part, about becoming a shelter for each other, a sanctuary and a place of rest.

I'd had a tough day at camp, getting stuck into all the activities before leading the evening Bible meeting with Pete. There'd been some emotionally big stuff that had come up throughout the week and the day, and at the end of it I just sat in the hall while other leaders listened to Disney music and played four square. I was praying desperately and ran out of the hall to read Psalm 8:1–4 in the quiet space under the stars:

> Lord, our Lord,
>   how majestic is your name in all the earth!
> You have set your glory
>   in the heavens.
> Through the praise of children and infants
>   you have established a stronghold against your enemies,
>   to silence the foe and the avenger.
> When I consider your heavens,
>   the work of your fingers,
> the moon and the stars,
>   which you have set in place,
> what is mankind that you are mindful of them,
>   human beings that you care for them?

I read and prayed this, the Spirit speaking to me in whispers without words about how God has ordained children to sing his praise and display his glory, about how he holds me in his hands even when I'm completely overwhelmed and knocked for six.

Five or so minutes later, I turned to re-enter the hall. Before I got there, Phil, another leader, met me and asked if I was all right – he'd noticed something was not quite okay. Although I tried to be brave and say I was okay (is this really bravery?), he saw right through it and put his arms around me and just prayed for peace. Peace that surpasses all understanding; wholeness that makes all things right again; joined-up-ness in the midst of the overwhelm.

I didn't know Phil super well – I'd only ever spent time with him on camp. Yet, in that moment, and throughout the rest of the week on camp, he looked out for me and listened when I couldn't quite make sense of it all myself. This is what church is to me: the place where God's precious people pray peace over each other, searching for wholeness, asking for grace to rain down.

It's like the men who carried the paralytic to Jesus to be healed (Luke 5:18–25, verse 18 in particular). Could this be us? Could church be this, a community raised up to support and believe truth for each other, to carry each other to Jesus so that we can receive his life, grow in holiness, and become characterised by his darkness-defying joy?

Yet, church isn't just a hospital and a sanctuary, there to offer rest and healing after the hurt has already happened. As church, we should be proactive as well as reactive, putting our best foot forward in extending the invitation of God's grace to every single person even before they realise they need it. We're here to bring God's kingdom right into the midst of this world, right into the midst of its politics and workings as we love practically and shine Christ's light that overcomes darkness. This happens as we both welcome in the world-weary *and* go out to seek and support all those who haven't yet heard God's voice, meeting each person's needs – both physically and spiritually.

It's captured in Isaiah 54:2: 'Enlarge the place of your tent, stretch your tent curtains wide, do not hold back; lengthen your cords, strengthen your stakes.' A couple of churches I've visited have adopted this as their vision statement, aiming to embrace the challenge God has for his church: open up your churches and invite people in; make wide and free your meeting places. Do not hold back – go after those who are in need of God's grace.

Go after those in need of grace: as church, as Christ's body, we are both a waiting sanctuary *and* a team of searchers, scanning the landscape for people to invite to sit at the table with us – *with* God – and find restoration and new life. As the widow hunted for the coin and the shepherd searched for the lost sheep; as the father of the prodigal ran out indecently to meet his son and as the king's servant searched the roads for people to invite to the banquet; as Jesus came down from heaven to earth to seek and save the lost – so we go, out on to our streets, into our schools and governments, industries and workplaces, homes and university halls, council estates and expensive apartments. So, we go and we search, shining light and bringing hope, extending the invitation and widening the curtains of our tent. Where is God calling you to go and to search? Who is he inviting you to bring into his presence?

Again, what shall we say the church is like? What parable should we use to describe it? We are like the mustard tree that springs up from the tiniest seed to become the biggest of all the garden plants: our branches unfurl as our roots go deep down in God's grace, and to our branches flock the birds. The birds flock – they are the lost and the lonely, the hungry and the thirsty, the happy and the curious, the ones freed from oppression and those still in chains. The people we attract might not be those we expect, and they might not be those we would naturally invite, but this is the beauty of being Christ's body. Every part is different and all parts are loved. All parts are equal – and all people are in need of grace. We as the church become those who invite people into grace precisely because we first received grace from God; and the invitation is extended both within our doors as we open the sanctuary, and without our doors as we widen our tent curtains, unfurl our branches and go to seek and save the lost.

This is my prayer and my hope for church community. I hope what I've written here has helped you to glimpse God's heart for what he longs for his people – even though they are words from just my one perspective. Take a few moments to think about what God's spoken to you about what church is and could be. There are some headphones questions below to help you think and pray through it all – why not gather some church friends and have these chats together?

Headphones time

- Return to the words you jotted down at the start of the previous chapter about church liturgy. Through reading the last two chapters, has anything about your view of church changed? If so, what? And if not, is there anything that has encouraged or challenged you from the last two chapters?

- A friend once sent me this quote: 'This world is not made of shades of grey. It is made of colours like azure and coral and emerald and marigold. But it insists on painting everything in black and white and fitting it into boxes that it understands. Do not do that to yourself. Paint your personality a million different colours.'[72] I find this so encouraging and freeing. None of us can be labelled and boxed up and still be free to be who God has created us to be. How can the church create space for people to be who they are? How can we become more accepting and unconditionally loving? Think of something you could do, either individually or with others in your church, to open wide the doors into God's family.

- Remember a time when you've felt really encouraged. Ask God to show you someone for whom you could be the encouragement. Resolve to encourage them, in whatever way is appropriate, over the next ten days.

- Read 2 Corinthians 6:16. What does it mean to be God's dwelling-place? How do you think the church is doing in remembering and living this?

- 'Has not God chosen those who are poor in the eyes of the world to be rich in faith and to inherit the kingdom he promised those who love him?' (James 2:5; for extra context see James 2:1–7). How does this challenge you about what inclusivity is?

Soundtrack

'Cathedrals' by Tenth Avenue North.

Listen to what this says about who we are as church.

It never fails to bear fruit

Problems are susceptible to solutions; mysteries can only be illuminated.[73]

The quote above is one of my favourite quotations. I found it while reading for an essay on Job, an essay which asked the question as to whether or not the book of Job offered any 'solution' to suffering. My conclusion rejected the premise of the question: suffering, and the whole purposes and workings of God, are not a 'problem' to be 'solved'. Rather, they are a mystery to be illuminated by the loving, powerful and trustworthy God – God, who brings us light even as we walk through the dark places, who helps us even as we struggle to persevere. We are called by the grace of God to keep trusting, to keep putting our roots deep down in him and to keep entering into the mystery and wonderful adventure of following him.

Indeed, mystery is embedded in the very word of God: he speaks to us in parables and images, stories to be entered into and explored, stories that make us think and understand as they reflect a million different glimmers of light from the person of Jesus.

One such image is the one we've returned to again and again throughout this book, from Jeremiah 17:7–8:

But blessed is the one who trusts in the Lord,
    whose confidence is in him.
They will be like a tree planted by the water
    that sends out its roots by the stream.

It does not fear when heat comes;
   its leaves are always green.
It has no worries in a year of drought,
   and never fails to bear fruit.

With this image beside us, we've explored different rhythms of rootedness – different ways that we can seek God's kingdom first and create space in our lives to listen to and be led by him. I hope you've found the stories and suggestions useful as you've thought about how you can live your faith in every moment, and as you've prayed through what God is inviting you to know and experience of him.

Further, I hope you've seen that it's impossible to talk about putting down roots in God's grace without also mentioning the fruit that this brings. We see it in those Jeremiah verses: roots lead on to fruit. Our roots are sent out by the stream; consequently, we will never fail to bear fruit.

We will never fail to bear fruit: we will always grow in grace and bring life to those around us. The work of God's love will always be evident as we put our roots down in him. We will become fearless under pressure; our leaves will be evergreen. We will be calm and confident even when we go through times of lack and struggle; fruit will surely grow amid adversity as we persevere. We will be strong in him, for he is strong even when we are weak. God is making 'a way in the wilderness and streams in the wasteland' (Isaiah 43:19) – new life springs up in his wake.

This verse from Isaiah came to life as I returned to Cambridge after Escape and Pray. Becca, who we'd met in Madrid, had encouraged us with those Isaiah-words, saying that each of us, as we travelled on from Spain, would become like streams in the desert, bringing life as we journeyed to new places. Fruit would grow as we trusted in God.

In the following 36 hours in Cambridge, I saw this happen repeatedly in the conversations I had. The evening I returned, I enjoyed a spontaneous dinner with Amy and Matt; we encouraged each other by telling stories of God's goodness. Walking back to our colleges, Matt and I stopped on Clare Bridge (which was lit up in bright pink ready for an extravagant party, the 'May Ball', happening there the day after); we chatted long about what God had been speaking to each of us, and we prayed before going home.

Back in my room, I saw my sparkly dress hanging up ready to wear to that extravagant ball – I felt funny about it because partying was so completely different to being on mission in Madrid. Yet as I looked, I felt God saying: 'Pilgrims can wear these clothes too.' True to his word, God was at the May Ball as much as he was in Madrid: I had an absolutely wonderful time with my friend Lizzie as we sat eating doughnuts at 1.00 am, wearing our fancy dresses, laughing and chatting about God, the life of faith and spirituality. I learned so much from her and really valued our conversation. She isn't a Christian, and nor are most people. Yet, God brings life and fruit in *every* circumstance and *every* conversation, longing to bring new life and love to every beating heart in this world. Thus, we never fail to bear fruit when our roots are in God's grace and we are open to his work in our lives. What stories do you have of God's surprising grace?

The fruit that God's grace brings is not just in surprising, everyday moments and opportunities. It's also in the character that grace produces in you, the person you become as you follow God's ways.

It's incredible, and only possible with him: he turns fearfulness to joy; worry to confidence; fear to boldness. Generosity and selfless love take the place of selfishness and pride; kindness reigns where there once was discord. Confidence and resilience characterise his people as they stand up for truth and justice; freedom breaks apart anything that once was a prison.

Jesus brings incredible transformation to those who encounter him and keep company with him – like Zacchaeus, who changed from being corrupt and selfish to truthful and generous (Luke 19:1–10);

like the crippled woman who, when healed by Jesus, was changed from broken and imprisoned to free and joyful (Luke 13:10–17); like every person who's heard Jesus speak and chosen to take hold of his grace. He refines our faith and character so that we come to reflect him more and more, distinctive in a world that does not always recognise him.

Despite how amazing all of this is, the greatest fruit and joy that comes from putting roots down in God's grace is simply this: that we get to know God. God – the Creator who's close enough to whisper and powerful enough to roar. The one who can hold the ocean in his hands; the one who's created galaxy upon galaxy too far away for us to see. The one whose power is thunderous and whose love is wild – so thunderous and wild that he gave his all to us in Jesus.

He has already given his all to us – and now he invites us to keep company with him, to keep opening the gift of his grace and to keep diving into the mystery of who he is.

C.S. Lewis phrases this continual journey wonderfully in *Prince Caspian*, part of the Narnia series. Lucy is reunited with the lion Aslan:

> 'Welcome child,' he said.
> 'Aslan,' said Lucy, 'you're bigger.'
> 'That is because you are older, little one,' answered he.
> 'Not because you are?'
> 'I am not. But every year you grow, you will find me bigger.'[74]

As she grows, Lucy finds Aslan bigger. She sees more of him – she understands more of the mystery of his character.

As we grow in rootedness and in grace, so we find God bigger. We see more of him – we understand more of the mystery of who he is and how he loves us.

This is the invitation for you as you finish reading this book. God knows and loves you completely, and he has made a way for you to be with him. He invites you into his presence, and he longs for you to know him more. How will you accept the invitation? How will you grow roots in his grace? Let us finish with the prayer with which we began.

Father, may your Spirit fill us with hunger for you.

Inspire us to pray with your passion, the joy of your presence motivating us and your will sustaining us. Let us lay down our own agendas and aims.

Give us fresh vision of the fruit you want to bring from our lives; teach us to be rooted deep in you and help us to make space to listen to you.

Make us radically confident in you; help us to know Jesus and joyfully follow his voice without comparing ourselves to others. May we keep our eyes fixed only on you as you write our stories.

Father, bring us to full, vibrant, world-changing life as we find ourselves in you.

In your everlasting, heart-beating-love, grace-running-wild name,

Amen

Recommendations

There are thousands of books, articles, blog posts and songs out there written to encourage, challenge and inspire you; to illuminate tricky issues or experiences; to reveal more of God's kind, powerful and infinite character. Below is a list of just some of the books, blog sites and music that I have enjoyed and learned from in the last couple of years. Go read and listen for yourself – you never know what you might discover.

Books

- Graham Beynon, *Experiencing the Spirit* (IVP, 2006)
- Enzo Bianchi, *God, Where are You?* (SPCK, 2014)*
- Steven Chase, *Nature as Spiritual Practice* (Eerdmans, 2011)
- Gordon D. Fee and Douglas Stuart, *How to Read the Bible for All its Worth* (Zondervan, 2003)*
- Richard Foster, *Celebration of Discipline* (Hodder & Stoughton, 2008)*
- Richard Foster, *Prayer* (Hodder & Stoughton, 1992)
- Emily P. Freeman, *A Million Little Ways* (Revell, 2013)
- Luigi Gioia, *Say it to God* (Bloomsbury, 2017)
- Lis Goddard and Clare Hendry, *The Gender Agenda* (IVP, 2010)
- Nell Goddard, *Musings of a Clergy Child* (BRF, 2017)
- Paula Gooder, *Let Me Go There* (Canterbury Press, 2016)*
- Pete Grieg, *Dirty Glory* (Navpress, 2016)
- Alan Hargrave, *One For Sorrow* (SPCK, 2017)
- W. Phillip Keller, *As a Tree Grows* (Zondervan, 2007)

- C.S. Lewis, *The Screwtape Letters* (Zondervan, 2001)
- Sally Lloyd-Jones, *The Jesus Storybook Bible* (Zondervan, 2012)
- Shauna Niequist, *Bittersweet* (Zondervan, 2013)
- J. I. Packer, *Knowing God* (Hodder & Stoughton, 2005)
- Matt Redman and Louie Giglio, *Indescribable* (David C. Cook, 2011)
- Jo Swinney, *God Hunting* (Scripture Union, 2011)*
- Ann Voskamp, *The Broken Way* (Zondervan, 2016)
- Rowan Williams, *The Lion's World* (SPCK, 2012)
- Rowan Williams, *Meeting God in Paul* (SPCK, 2015)*
- Philip Yancey, *What's So Amazing About Grace?* (Zondervan, 2002)

* These books are particularly helpful for answering some of your big questions about the Bible: why it is like it is and how to engage with different genres in the Bible.

Blogs and websites

- **More Precious**, www.moreprecious.co.uk
  This is a site aimed at teenage girls and women. It's packed full of posts, resources and videos to help you pursue God and flourish as his daughter – check it out to find out more!

- **threads (UK)**, www.threadsuk.com
  threads is a collective of curious Christians. Here, you'll find posts on a wide range of head-scratching and deeply relevant topics.

- **A Holy Experience**, www.aholyexperience.com
  A Holy Experience is the online dwelling of Ann Voskamp, passionate Jesus-follower and author. Her posts are deep, reflective and always full of life-giving wisdom and insight into how we can walk by faith and not by sight.

- **Chatter and Scribblings**, chatterandscribblings.wordpress.com
  Katherine says: 'Hello! I'm Katherine, a student who loves Jesus, stories and the moments where they meet. My little blog is a corner

of the internet where I try to link up God's truths to the world I'm living in at university. Sometimes it's a way to offer glimpses of the gospel to my friends through culture or the news. Other times it's just an honest reflection on how things are going in the joyful and heart-breaking moments of this wonderfully messy now.'

- **The Joy of Rachel**, www.thejoyofrachel.com
Rachel says: 'E.L. Doctorow said of writing, "It's like driving at night with the headlights on. You can only see a little way ahead of you, but you can make the whole journey that way."' My blog fits that description. When I look back over it, I see the journey I've been going on in a way that I don't in the moment of each post. You'll find that the things I write are of a very assorted nature – thoughts and photos of travel and friends, reflections on hard things and good things; on life and faith in the intertwined way that they are. I'd love for you to share in it all.'

- **musingsofaclergychild**, www.alianore.co.uk
This is the blog site of the wonderful Nell Goddard whose book, *Musings of a Clergy Child* (BRF, 2017), is such a joy, encouragement and challenge to read. Check out the site to keep up-to-date with what she's musing about.

- **Tearfund Lifestyle**, lifestyle.tearfund.org
Here, you'll find all sorts of posts, tips and ideas about how we can love mercy, seek justice and walk humbly with our God. Christ-centred social justice inspired by compassion for all is at the core of Tearfund's ministry as they 'follow Jesus where the need is greatest'.

- **CreatedEnough**, createdenough.wordpress.com
This is my own blog, so it's perhaps a little cheeky to put it on the recommendations list! Check it out if you'd like to keep up with what I'm writing. Through my posts I hope to explore how wide, deep and long is God's grace, through everyday experiences, encounters and stories.

Music

Albums

- All Sons and Daughters, 'Poets and Saints'
- Andrew Peterson, 'Counting Stars' and 'Light for the Lost Boy'
- Bethel, 'You Make Me Brave', 'Without Words' and 'Synesthesia'
- Gungor, 'Beautiful Things'
- Kari Jobe, 'The Garden'
- Leeland, 'Invisible'
- Rend Collective, 'Good News'
- Tenth Avenue North, 'Followers' and 'Cathedrals'
- Young Oceans, 'Voices, Vol. 1' and 'Steady the Stars'

Chapter soundtracks

- Matt Redman (feat. Tasha Cobbs Leonard), 'Gracefully broken'
- Sanctus Real, 'Whatever you're doing'
- Kari Jobe, 'The garden'
- Rend Collective, 'Whatever comes'
- Holy Trinity Worship, 'Your ways'
- Sojourn Music, 'Come ye sinners'
- David Crowder, 'Come as you are'
- Hans Zimmer, 'Planet Earth II suite'
- David Evans, 'Be still for the presence of the Lord'
- Tenth Avenue North, 'Overflow'
- Tenth Avenue North, 'Cathedrals'

Finally: I would love to meet you! If you'd like me to speak or run a workshop at your church or youth group, based around themes from *Rooted in God's Grace* or *God's Daughters*, get in touch with me by messaging me through my Facebook page: www.facebook.com/ createdenough. I look forward to hearing from you!

Notes

1. G.K. Chesterton, in Sally Lloyd-Jones, *The Jesus Storybook Bible* (Zondervan, 2012), p. 11.
2. Matt Redman and Louie Giglio, *Indescribable* (David C. Cook, 2011), pp. 43–44.
3. Redman and Giglio, *Indescribable*, pp. 89–90.
4. Emphasis mine.
5. For a more in-depth look at this Greek phrase, see Emily P. Freeman, *A Million Little Ways* (Revell, 2013), pp. 24–27.
6. Sheridan Voysey, 'He knows you', www.threadsuk.com/he-knows-you, accessed 2 August 2017.
7. Philip Yancey, *What's So Amazing About Grace?* (Zondervan, 2002), p. 13.
8. Darrell L. Bock, *The NIV Application Commentary: Luke* (Zondervan, 1996), p. 230.
9. J. Louis Martyn, *Galatians* (Doubleday, 1997), p. 229.
10. Dallas Willard, 'Live life to the full', www.dwillard.org/articles/artview.asp?artID=5, accessed 24 August 2017.
11. Willard, 'Live life to the full'.
12. Richard Foster, *Celebration of Discipline* (Hodder & Stoughton, 2008), p. 8.
13. Isaac of Nineveh, in Robert Atwell (ed.), *Celebrating the Seasons: Daily spiritual readings for the Christian year* (Canterbury Press, 1999), p. 296.
14. If you'd like to learn more about the Escape and Pray experience, visit: www.fusionmovement.org/escapeandpray.
15. Why a Red Box? Check it out: eng.ontheredbox.com.
16. Graham Beynon, *Experiencing the Spirit* (IVP, 2006), p. 71.
17. Ann Voskamp, 'When you are weary of vanilla Christianity', www.annvoskamp.com/2013/01/when-you-are-weary-of-vanilla-Christianity, accessed 2 August 2017.
18. Pete Greig in Jo Swinney, *God Hunting* (Scripture Union, 2011), p. 32.
19. Jill Weber, 'Start strong: awake to his presence', www.24-7prayer.com/blog/2656/start-strong-awake-to-his-presence, accessed 27 August 2017.
20. Swinney, *God Hunting*, p. 33.
21. This refers to the Isthmian games, a bit like the Olympic games, that were held every two years in Corinth.

22 Alan Hargrave, *One For Sorrow* (SPCK, 2017), p. 74.

23 Swinney, *God Hunting*, p. 107.

24 As an aside, another friend of mine, Lucy, wrote a blog post for a university event all about her story with God through anorexia. You'll find it here: justlovecambridge.wordpress.com/2017/05/07/flourish-restored. It's an amazing testimony to God's love, kindness and power, and well worth a read whether you're thinking through these issues or not.

25 Emma Rutter, 'Control', cooking-in-cashmere.blogspot. co.uk/2017/08/control.html, accessed 2 August 2017.

26 Gandalf, in *The Hobbit: An Unexpected Journey* (2012), Peter Jackson (Warner Bros. Pictures).

27 Allison, 'I am average', www.agirlikeme.com/i-am-average, accessed 2 August 2017.

28 Hargrave, *One For Sorrow*, p. 73.

29 I also wrote about these experiences as they happened, over at my blog: www.createdenough.wordpress.com.

30 'To boldly go wherever darkness needs to be overcome' was a catchphrase at camp – all credit for the phrase to Liz Howden.

31 Shauna Niequist, *Bittersweet* (Zondervan, 2013), p. 13.

32 Ann Voskamp, *The Broken Way* (Zondervan, 2016), p. 26.

33 Hargrave, *One For Sorrow*, p. 77.

34 Lloyd-Jones, *The Jesus Storybook Bible*, p. 12.

35 Rachel Mander, '8 Months, 1 Journal', www.thejoyofrachel. com/2017/05/03/8-months-1-journal, accessed 15 August 2017.

36 Hargrave, *One For Sorrow*, pp. 72–73.

37 If you're curious, the commentaries Stu used are these: Gordon J. Wenham, *The Book of Leviticus* (Eerdmans, 1979) and Nobuyoshi Kiuchi, *Leviticus (Apollos Old Testament Commentary)*, (IVP Academic, 2007). He says that they're great but not very accessible – they're for you if you'd like to be challenged and stretched theologically.

38 Margaret White, 'Faith Worked Out: Margaret White', www. moreprecious.co.uk/blog/2015/03/14/margaret-white, accessed 31 July 2017.

39 You can find the sermon ('The need to stay hungry' by Oli Benyon) and the series it belongs to here (it's a good one!): www. htcambridge.org.uk/fulfilled-living-in-8-steps.

40 Lloyd-Jones, *The Jesus Storybook Bible*, p. 227.

41 Richard Foster, *Prayer* (Hodder & Stoughton, 1992), p. 3.
42 Foster, *Prayer*, pp. 1–3.
43 Hannah Fytche, *God's Daughters* (BRF, 2016), p. 99.
44 Jeffrey Guille, 'Psalm 23 – David's heavenly pastoral (1)', jeffreyguille. blogspot.co.uk/2016/07/psalm-23-davids-heavenly-pastoral-1.html, accessed 15 August 2017.
45 W. Phillip Keller, *A Shepherd Looks at Psalm 23* (Zondervan, 2007).
46 Beynon, *Experiencing the Spirit*, p. 70.
47 Foster, *Prayer*, p. 5.
48 Shout-out to Nathan for remembering the exact song three months after we'd sung it!
49 C.S. Lewis, in Hargrave, *One For Sorrow*, p. 62.
50 Steven Chase, *Nature as Spiritual Practice* (Eerdmans, 2011), p. 25.
51 www.poetryfoundation.org/poets/gerard-manley-hopkins, accessed 31 July 2017.
52 I quoted this in *God's Daughters*: 'Why must people kneel down to pray? If I really wanted to pray, I'll tell you what I'd do. I'd go out into a great big field all alone or into the deep, deep woods, and I'd look up into the sky – up – up – up – into that lovely blue sky that looks as if there was no end to its blueness. And then I'd just *feel* a prayer.' L.M. Montgomery, *Anne of Green Gables* (Puffin Books 1977), p. 47.
53 Chase, *Nature as Spiritual Practice*, p. 12.
54 G.K. Chesterton, in Chase, *Nature as Spiritual Practice*, p. 38.
55 Robert Macfarlane, *The Old Ways* (Penguin, 2013), p. 18.
56 Foster, *Celebration of Discipline*, p. 122.
57 Hargrave, *One For Sorrow*, p. 81.
58 Marilynne Robinson, *Home* (Virago Press, 2009), p. 115.
59 Mike Donehey, *We are Cathedrals Devotional* – a devotional booklet based on the songs from Tenth Avenue North's 'Cathedrals' album. See tenthavenuenorth.store/products/we-are-cathedrals-devotional-pre-order.
60 You can read more about the chapel and choir at Clare College by visiting this website: www.clare.cam.ac.uk/Chapel-and-Choir. Have a listen to some of the music – does this help you to worship God?
61 Paula Gooder has written some very good devotional books that take you through the different seasons of the Christian year. Find them here: www.gooder.me.uk/books.
62 Listen here: www.youtube.com/watch?v=4lC7V8hG198.
63 Hannah Fytche, 'Ashes and new life', createdenough.wordpress. com/2017/03/03/ashes-and-new-life, accessed 29 August 2017.

64   Foster, *Celebration of Discipline*, p. 198.

65   BBC Radio 4 *Sunday Worship* (19 February 2017), www.bbc.co.uk/
     programmes/b08fdhjq, accessed 26 February 2017.

66   Album title, Rend Collective (August 2015).

67   Stephen Gaukroger and Derek Wood, *Discovering Colossians and
     Philemon* (Crossway Books, 2002), p. 79.

68   This is a very brief way to mention my opinion on the complex
     theological issue of women in leadership – and I realise that it leaves
     much to be desired as an explanation or discussion about how I've
     arrived at this belief. I can point you to two excellent resources which
     have helped me to think through questions of gender roles and
     biblical leadership: Lis Goddard and Clare Hendry's book *The Gender
     Agenda* (Inter-Varsity Press, 2010) which explores the debate from
     both sides; and the website www.juniaproject.com, which exists in
     order to advocate 'for the inclusion of women in leadership in the
     Christian church'.

69   See www.gallupstrengthscenter.com.

70   W. Phillip Keller, *As a Tree Grows* (Billy Graham Evangelistic
     Association, 1966), pp. 17–18.

71   I guess he might have borrowed this image from Pope Francis: 'The
     thing the church needs most today is the ability to heal wounds and
     to warm the hearts of the faithful; it needs nearness, proximity. I see
     the church as a field hospital after battle.' www.ncronline.org/blogs/
     francis-chronicles/pope-s-quotes-field-hospital-church, accessed 18
     August 2017.

72   Nikita Gill, meanwhilepoetry.tumblr.com/post/139511054133/this-
     world-is-not-made-of-shades-of-grey-it-is, accessed 18 August 2017.

73   James L. Crenshaw, 'When form and content clash: the theology of
     Job 38:1—40:5', in *Urgent Advice and Probing Questions: Collected
     writings on Old Testament wisdom* (Mercer University Press, 1995),
     p. 465.

74   C.S. Lewis, *Prince Caspian* (Harper Collins, 2001), p. 155.

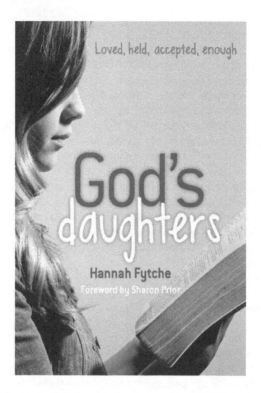

In this book, Hannah takes six issues, each of which comes with its own pressures: school, image, friends, family, church and our personal relationships with God. In each case, we may feel that our teachers, family, friends or even God expects us to be better than we feel inside. We may feel that, if we don't meet these expectations, we need to work harder in order to be loved and accepted. But this is not true! We need to let God strengthen us to keep walking. We need to listen to his gentle voice – and be encouraged to lift our eyes to him and dwell in his amazing grace.

God's Daughters
Loved, held, accepted, enough
Hannah Fytche
978 0 85746 409 5 £6.99

brfonline.org.uk

musings of a clergy child
growing into a faith of my own

Nell Goddard

Vicarage life can be exciting, hilarious, scary, surreal and delightful... and that's just one day! Nell Goddard writes honestly and openly about the ins and outs of growing up in a Christian home, from her experience as the daughter of two vicars. With both rewritten blog posts and brand new material, this collection of tips, letters and musings will appeal not just to clergy children and their parents, but also to teenagers growing up in Christian homes, and to those who want to know what it's like to live a life of ministry you never really asked for.

Musings of a Clergy Child
Growing into a faith of my own
Nell Goddard
978 0 85746 546 7 £7.99

brfonline.org.uk

BRF

Transforming
lives and communities

Christian growth and understanding of the Bible

Resourcing individuals, groups and leaders in churches for their own spiritual journey and for their ministry

Church outreach in the local community

Offering three programmes that churches are embracing to great effect as they seek to engage with their local communities and transform lives

Teaching Christianity in primary schools

Working with children and teachers to explore Christianity creatively and confidently

Children's and family ministry

Working with churches and families to explore Christianity creatively and bring the Bible alive

Visit **brf.org.uk** for more information on BRF's work

brf.org.uk